1-30-75

THE POLITICS
OF TRADE

After a brief survey of the post-war economic order and its evolution from the Bretton Woods era of U.S. primacy to the current emerging five-power system of the United States, the Soviet Union, the EEC, Japan and China, the introduction warns that the currently high level of interdependence between the industrialized countries could be threatened by the emergence of the superblocs described in detail in the main part of the book. Pointing out that economic regionalism has already become seriously entrenched the introduction spells out the underlying aim of the book is to provide an analysis of the relationship between power politics and the drift to protectionism in world trade.

The first chapter of the book deals with the history of protectionism in the twentieth century and is a timely reminder that protectionism is the rule rather than the exception in the modern world. The second chapter enunciates a new geopolitical theory, that of economic multipolarity (or the doctrine of the superbloc) which baldly stated suggests that when you have a given number of major world concentrations of economic power whose influence embraces the entire world there will exist a built-in tendency toward conflict if only because the superblocs which arise can only expand or maintain their relative strength at the expense of or by excluding the other superblocs. In effect, the advent of the superbloc appears likely to reinforce protectionism.

The major part of the book is devoted to a detailed documentation of the world-wide effects of the original Common Market Six and how it has helped to

continued on the back flap

shape the new multipolar five-power system. First there is a description of the Eurafrican bloc which appears to be evolving, linking ever more closely, for good or ill, most of Western Europe with the Mediterranean littoral and prospectively much of Anglophile as well as Francophobe Africa. Second, there is a description of the Soviet Union's development as a Eurasian power, consolidating her economic stranglehold in Eastern Europe and advancing her claim to the general overlordship of most of continental South Asia (Pakistan excepted). Third, there is an examination of the delicate and increasingly fractious relationship between the United States and Latin America. Fourthly and fifthly there are separate chapters on the re-emergence of both Japan and China as world economic powers with their own respective spheres of influence. Finally Britain's relative position in the world economic system is assessed. There is a brief set of general conclusions of the key targets for reform in the international system.

THE POLITICS OF TRADE

THE EVOLUTION OF THE SUPERBLOC

Douglas Evans

A HALSTED PRESS BOOK

JOHN WILEY & SONS
New York - Toronto

First published in the United Kingdom 1974 by
The Macmillan Press Ltd

Published in the U.S.A. and
Canada by Halsted Press, a
Division of John Wiley & Sons, Inc.,
New York.

Library of Congress Cataloging in Publication Data

Evans, Douglas.
   The politics of trade.

   "A Halsted Press book."
   1. Commerce. 2. Monetary policy. 3. Commercial
policy. I. Title.
HF1007.E84   382.1   74-1183
ISBN 0-470-24881-5

Printed in Great Britain

Contents

Acknowledgements

It must be said at the outset that in the compilation of this book the documentation came first, followed by the enunciation of a general theory and conclusions. Without such detailed evidence there could be neither theory nor conclusions. Most of the sources for the evidence surveyed have been official government statistics made available by individual governments with the help and advice of a large number of Economic Counsellors without whose willing assistance it would not have been possible to write this book.

In addition I am indebted to Peter Tulloch of the Overseas Development Institute for the section on the Commonwealth Asian group of seven; also to Arturo O'Connell of the University of Santiago for the section on Latin America and to Peter Oppenheimer of Oxford University for the appendix on monetary reform. For the book as a whole I am indebted for his general advice to Brian Griffiths of the London School of Economics and for his general influence on my thinking to Professor Harry Johnson of the University of Chicago and London School of Economics. Neither of the latter should be held responsible for the views expressed in the book. Finally, I must thank my agent, Andrew Best of Curtis Brown, who encouraged me to believe that there was a book to be written and my editor at Macmillan, T. M. Farmiloe, who successfully nursed the project through to its publication. Also to Vivienne Asher, who typed the manuscript, and to H. W. Bawden and the Macmillan Press without whose forebearance the postscript and at least one appendix would not have been included.

Introduction: The Advent of the Superbloc

Thirty years ago the Bretton Woods monetary conference, later reinforced by the Marshall Plan, ushered in an era of prosperity and co-operation between the industrialised countries of the Western world. The Smithsonian Agreement of 1971 marked not only the end of the Bretton Woods monetary system but the end of an era of American leadership which had remained virtually unchallenged until that point. In the spring of 1973 Dr Kissinger's creative attempt to tackle the whole spectrum of trade, monetary and defence questions in a new Atlantic Charter between the United States, the European Economic Community and Japan, almost certainly designed as a tactical move to prod the Europeans to agreeing on a minimum common policy statement, was quietly rebuffed. Even though the threads were soon taken up again the whole affair illustrates the delicate nature of the multipolar economic system in which several centres of world power are emerging, namely the United States, the Soviet Union, the EEC, Japan and China, of whom the first two are also superpowers. Almost unnoticed these five centres of power have already staked out for themselves regions contiguous with themselves where the countries concerned are likely to behave more and more like economic satellites. This trend has given rise to a new phenomenon in world affairs which I have designated the superbloc — i.e. a unit comprising a great power (not necessarily a superpower) and its attendant economic satellites.

After a generation of living under a balance of terror system in which two superpowers exercised the right of most major world initiatives as well as shouldering the matching responsibilities to maintain a form of peace, most observers have welcomed the prospect of a new 'concert of the world'. However, the demands which such a system makes on the great powers concerned has not yet been fully assessed. Certainly in the field of economic relations the degree of responsibility, not to say cohesion, shown by some of the prospective great powers has not been of the sort to inspire confidence in a global concert of nations.

Taking full account of the advent of the superbloc the underlying aim of this book is to provide an analysis of the relationship between power politics and the drift to protectionism in world trade. Economic regionalism has already become seriously entrenched and it is all too easy to assume that the general prosperity which the industrialised world has enjoyed for the last thirty years will continue automatically.

It is now more than thirty-five years since the world last experienced a protectionist dominated world economic system and we have grown accustomed to living under a liberally orientated world economic order. We should remind ourselves that historically speaking there have been only relatively short periods when the world has enjoyed the benefits of a relatively liberal system. Even a brief survey of modern history confirms that protectionism in some shape or form is the rule rather than the exception. Furthermore, we should not be surprised if protectionism, which we have previously mentally discarded as a product of the 1930s, rears its head again in a new guise which broadly fits the description of modern mercantilism, sometimes labelled the new mercantilism. For in spite of the fact that the need for a liberal system of international trade has been seen to be universally desirable since the days of the early classical economists protectionist instincts have always persisted like some economic equivalent of original sin.

But if the irrationality of protectionism in trade has been generally acknowledged by political and economic theorists for some considerable time the need for a well-functioning international monetary system was only recognised following the breakdown of the gold standard system by the First World War and the economic collapse of the inter-war years.

It is the aim of this book to present evidence to demonstrate the current interaction between the world economic system in its trade and monetary aspects and the political interests of the great powers which has led to the emergence of the superblocs.

1 The History of Modern Protectionism*

In the nineteenth century the world economy was centred on Britain, the unchallenged pioneer of the Industrial Revolution. While Britain had plentiful coal and iron resources to support her manufacturing, her available agricultural land was limited. This fact coupled with her manufacturing supremacy led her quite painlessly to adopt a policy of free trade. Such a policy was not only ideal for Britain's own economic development but it also guaranteed that the process of economic development was transmitted to the rest of the world. This took place through the investment of British capital and the migration of British people to develop the external supplies of foodstuffs and raw materials that Britain's industrial growth increasingly demanded. This human and capital migration extended to North and South America, Australia, New Zealand and South Africa. Britain was at that moment the world's leading manufacturer, exporter of manufactures and importer of foodstuffs and materials, not to mention the principal provider of capital for the finance of world trade (in effect a sterling standard system).

With the deceleration of British industrial growth after about 1870, and the industrial development of countries with considerably richer natural resources, such as the United States, Germany and France, Britain's central role in the world economy began to decline. These changes were gradually absorbed over the next forty years until it was shattered by the outbreak and general consequences flowing from the Great War.

There is a good deal of truth in the claim that war is the ultimate experience of protection, certainly the First World War left a heavy legacy of increased protection. Not only did protection of industrial products increase — Britain breached

*The first half of this chapter has drawn extensively from *The World Economy at the Crossroads*, Harry G. Johnson, Oxford University Press, 1965.

her traditional policies of free trade on defence grounds —
but the European countries took steps to protect their
farmers from cheap grain imports from North and South
America, Australia and South Africa. The United States, which
emerged from the War as the world's premier industrial power
and could have taken Britain's place by moving towards freer
trade, had by 1930 adopted the strongly protectionist
Smoot-Hawley tariff. Increased protectionsim was also re-
flected in the United States by stricter immigration laws
marking the first major restraints she had ever imposed on
international labour mobility.

It should be noted that the entry of the United States into
the First World War in 1917 was a major turning-point in
history, marking a decisive stage in the transition from the
European age to the age of world politics. After the Bolshevik
revolution in Russia in November 1917 the world was for the
first time divided into two great rival power blocs, inspired
by apparently irreconcilable ideologies. The bipolar world
system had already begun to take shape. In spite of their
rivalry President Wilson and Lenin had one thing in common;
both rejected the existing international system including trade
discrimination and the then current balance of power in Europe.

More immediately and more seriously than the growth of
protectionism was the failure to re-establish a stable
international monetary system. It was attempted to re-
establish the pre-war gold standard but in the event the
pound was overvalued and the franc undervalued; and the
post-war extension of the gold standard to many more
countries than had previously been on it gave rise to a
demand for gold greater than the available stocks, which was
satisfied temporarily by the development of the gold exchange standard. The overvaluation of the pound made
Britain chronically depressed and economically stagnant,
with a serious retarding effect on economic growth elsewhere; it also made the preservation of the value of sterling
dependent on commanding sufficient foreign deposits.

By now Britain was no longer the unique centre of
the international financial and monetary system which was
now multi-centred with the United States newly emerged as a
major banking centre. It was a shaky system, dependent on

widespread holding of national currencies as a substitute for non-existent gold, and hence vulnerable to speculative international movements of capital, and it had to survive in a world fraught with national and international political tensions. It was set up and kept functioning in the 1920s by collaboration between the world's two strongest central banks, the Bank of England and the U.S. Federal Reserve; but central bank collaboration was insufficient to prevent its collapse in 1931. In the wake of the Great Crash and Great Depression came a period of severe monetary disorganisation. From such chaos each country attempted to rescue itself by resort to greatly increased protection combined with preferential and bilateral trading arrangements. The total result of this was a violent constriction of the volume and the seizing up of most of the channels of international trade.

When the Second World War ended and the opportunity for reconstructing the world economy arose, the experience of the 1930s was very much in the mind of the world's international economic experts. The Bretton Woods conference produced the major new institutions which were to last, more or less, up until the present time.

Those institutions included:

(1) The International Monetary Fund, to supplement the world's inadequate gold supply by credit facilities and to promote orderly adjustment of balance of payments disequilibria;

(2) an International Trade Organisation subsequently replaced by the General Agreement on Tariffs and Trade to guarantee non-discriminatory practices in commercial policy and to serve as an agency for negotiating the liberalisation of trade;

(3) an International Bank for Reconstruction and Development (now called the World Bank) to channel long-term capital to international investment in a steadier and more regular flow than private capital markets had previously provided. All these were designed to avoid the problems of the 1930s and have in consequence been only imperfectly adapted to the problems of the post-war world.

By the mid-1960s the Bretton Woods system was still working but beginning to show signs of some serious rifts. By 1964, when the first conference of UNCTAD (United Nations Conference on Trade and Development) met at Geneva, there was the shape of at least three major politically orientated groups. They were:

(1) the Anglo-Saxon group (led by the United States);
(2) the EEC (led by France);
(3) the Developing Countries (led by Dr Raul Prebisch).

At the risk of oversimplifying, the Anglo-Saxon group believed that the status quo could be maintained and modified. The French led EEC believed that a new system was desirable and that U.S. dominance should be reduced. In economic terms it was a conflict between multilateralism and most favoured nation treatment versus preferential trading arrangements. Above all the EEC represented the subordination of the economic view of the nature of competition in international trade to a political one. The Third World group was also opposed to the status quo in which they remained not only subordinate but depressed. GATT was regarded as being of the old order of things since it believed in reciprocity as a general basic principle and it seemed incapable of tackling agricultural trade. The Third World favoured UNCTAD because it gave them numerical power to wield for the first time. It proved incapable of overcoming the economic disequalities. This group, believing profoundly in making the developed world compensate for colonialism, represents a highly politicised view of the international economic system. Following the success of the Kennedy Round of international tariff reductions in the latter half of the 1960s the world once again turned towards the task of greater trade liberalisation in the 1970s through the forum of GATT.

The Liberalisation of Trade

The Tokyo ministerial meeting of GATT, held in September 1973, achieved the relatively modest goal of laying down the political guidelines for the 1974-75 Geneva trade negotiations between 100 countries. While the Tokyo declaration pledges the signatories to aim at the expansion and liberalisation of world trade and the securing of new benefits for the developing countries, the road to fulfilment of these lofty intentions is fraught with major conflicts of interest and approach, notably between the U.S. and the EEC.

While the Dillon and Kennedy Rounds were chiefly preoccupied with traditional tariff barriers the Nixon Round will be much more concerned with non-tariff barriers, agriculture and safeguards for domestic producers generally. This stems from the fact that thanks to previous trade rounds tariffs are sufficiently low as to have very little influence on the total volume of world trade. In 1972, for instance, world trade grew in value by 17 per cent due chiefly to a growth in trade volume of 10 per cent which hardly suggests that tariffs present insuperable obstacles to trade in industrial goods where most of the growth took place. In the same year the trade of developing countries grew in value by only 13 per cent, further reducing their share of total world trade.

Thus surveying the prospect in the four main fields of tariffs, non-tariff barriers, agriculture and safeguards we can safely anticipate a bitter and protracted struggle in the negotiations. In the field of traditional tariffs Japan and the U.S. broadly argue that since they are of minimal importance in affecting the trade flows they should be abolished completely. The Europeans, and especially the French, are unwilling since they see the abolition of the EEC's Common External Tariff as the removal of one of the twin pillars of the European Community as it currently exists (the other pillar is of course the CAP). In the case of non-tariff barriers, the greatest growth point in trade restrictions in recent years, there is likely to be the beginnings of a long, hard struggle which will continue long after the Geneva talks are due to be concluded at the end of 1975.

Safeguards are a major issue, largely as a result of some of the domestic industries adversely affected by the Kennedy Round cuts. How important they will loom can be seen in the clauses of the U.S. Trade Expansion Bill which leaves the President free to lower *or raise* tariffs at his own discretion to meet the needs of the moment. Last, but certainly not least, there is the vexed question of trade in agricultural goods which proved too hot a subject for the Kennedy Round to tackle effectively. At this point the French are adamantly opposed to discussing world trade in agriculture on the grounds that it is too socially important to submit to outside requirements. Since the evidence surveyed in this book suggests that EEC agricultural policy is the single most pervasive piece of legislation affecting world trade it can hardly be made an exception without making the trade negotiations largely meaningless.

Indeed, it is one of the underlying themes of this book that, despite the gratifying growth in world trade, if economic regionalism is allowed to develop without substantial mutual concessions in the fields under review in Geneva then a spate of protectionist measures and counter measures could very easily break out. After almost three decades of growing economic interdependence nobody can safely predict how harmful the effects would turn out to be. The only safe prediction is that no single country could conceivably benefit from such a development, which is not to say that it couldn't happen. The Geneva talks pose great technical problems but the underlying nature of these issues remains political. How can conflicting political interests come together to create an arrangement which will maximise the global economic benefits and at the same time deprive the least number. This is the only justification for discussing such issues within a political framework.

While it is probably inevitable that both the trade and monetary negotiations will be carried out largely between the great powers and the relatively small number of industrialized middle powers this book attempts to show how not only the major nations but also the smaller states are likely to be affected.

2 The Theory of Economic Multipolarity

If the existence of massive nuclear arsenals has reduced the likelihood of an outright war between the superpowers it does not remove the traditional political conflicts which inevitably arise between great powers. Whereas in the past these rivalries tended to be settled on the field, on the high seas and in the air, now they are likely to be fought out, or averted, in the sphere of international economic and commercial policies. This conflict has to a considerable extent superseded the clear-cut ideological conflict between Communist and non-Communist powers since effectively both are pursuing commercial policies dictated by national political objectives. Thus the conflict between the Soviet Union and China arises not simply because two Communist states have reached different stages in their economic development and have evolved separate modes of Communism, but also because of their very similarity of scale combined with conflicting ambitions in the same areas. This is apparent not only on the Mongolian border but throughout much of continental Asia, which both aspire to dominate. The principle of a clash of interest for geopolitical rather than ideological reasons is hardly a new concept. What is a relatively new development is that this geopolitical conflict of interest between the great powers is for perhaps the very first time in history literally a global phenomenon. That is, the conflict of interest between the great powers, through the agency of the superbloc, involves each and every country in the world.

Though it is discreetly veiled with invocations of past and present alliances and genuine common concerns, the conflict between the United States and the EEC contains geopolitical rivalries potentially, if not yet actually, comparable in scale to the Sino-Soviet dispute. Like the differences between the Russians and the Chinese the conflict between the Atlantic partners derives from significantly different historical experiences. To take an important example, the highly different experiences of the United States, France and Germany during the Great Depression have greatly influenced their underlying approach to monetary questions not only at the level of their respective treasuries but also in the attitudes of the responsible political figures. Where the United States (and Britain) experienced massive and prolonged unemployment the Franco-German national consciousness was indelibly branded with the memory of uncontrolled inflation. Not surprisingly, in monetary affairs, the United States has tended to be obsessed with the need to avoid unnecessary unemployment while in Germany, and possibly to a lesser extent in France, there is an almost pathological fear of uncontrolled inflation. It is profound historical influences of this sort which at once sear a nation's folk memory and set the tone for its social priorities, creating differences in political attitudes from which the seemingly merely technical differences of approach on matters such as exchange rate adjustments ultimately spring.

Given that the American experience and the Continental European one were so different it has always seemed predictable that when the EEC became large and strong enough it would challenge the United States at those points where their traditional interests and policies clashed, as in agriculture. The fact that France (rather than Germany or Britain) has assumed the leadership of Western Europe has made this apparent even earlier than might otherwise have been the case. There are of course readily identifiable theoretical and practical reasons why, in common with most advanced industrialised countries, both the United States and France have at different periods heavily protected their agricultural sectors. Chief among these reasons are the immobility of labour off the land and the 'immobility' of agricultural land, that is the difficulty of converting such previously labour intensive land into other profitable uses. If we can identify general theoretical reasons why a particular sector of the economy finds it necessary to invoke protection in some shape or form it would seem reasonable to attempt to discover a general political theory which would explain the propensity towards protectionism which is documented in this book and seems to be endemic in the mid-1970s.

While there are usually readily identifiable immediate reasons for protectionism — the securing, maintenance or expansion of employment provides the classic and commonest justification — there are also long-term and much less easily identifiable reasons. In the debate which takes place constantly between national governments it is these latter underlying forces which tend to be overlooked, not least because they take place gradually and are rarely expressed in terms of public policy statements. Most commonly the forces which provide the driving force in modern protectionism arise from one of two sources. Either they evolve more or less consciously from a set of general assumptions about the nature of power politics which demands a continual increase in aggregate national wealth, or alternatively they arise almost unconsciously as a cumulative consequence of the pursuit of domestic policies without reference to external economic interests. Neither of these sources of modern protectionism is mutually exclusive. Indeed, it is when both forces are working together that the drive towards protectionism becomes most potent and sustained. When such forces exist together and are allowed to develop gradually over a period of years — up to a decade for instance — they rather naturally become entrenched. Traditionally in such circumstances the need to continue to satisfy the expectations of those employed in protected industries provides the popular pressure in the form of political and financial muscle to pursue national political goals based on the crudest of mercantilist assumptions.

In recent times, however, with the significant shift in power in the modern mixed capitalist economies from parliamentary and governmental institutions towards the multinational company, the need to acquire popular support for mercantilist policies has become increasingly less important. It is generally realised that the multinational company, as we shall outline in a moment, has contributed substantially to the size and nature of world trade in the 1960s and 1970s. What is now becoming evident is that in the future the multinational company could become the spearhead of the fast-evolving Western superblocs — that is the United States, Japan and the EEC. While the EEC owes much of its growth to American multinationals in Europe — two-thirds of American post-war overseas direct investment has been to Western Europe — there is considerable resistance to their operations. The EEC Commission has already begun to formulate a policy on multinationals which is clearly de-signed to limit U.S. multinationals and deter Japanese multinationals while fostering the growth of Common Market multinationals in their stead. While about one-fifth of America's 1,000 largest corporations conduct more than 50 per cent of their business abroad there is likely to be strong pressure for U.S. multinationals to concentrate either at home or in Latin America. Even though about one-tenth of America's 500 largest companies are heavily dependent on defence contracts they are likely to have less influence on the shaping of foreign policy as time goes on and the multi-nationals as a whole assume a preponderant role in the foreign policy of the Western superblocs. But before examining what the future political influence of the multinationals may turn out to be, it is worth looking at the overall trade patterns in which the multinational companies have already played such a significant part.

Industrialised Trade and the Multinationals

For very nearly twenty years there has been a steadily accelerating growth in trade and investment flows with an accompanying exchange of technological and managerial skills, between the advanced industrial countries.* The two

---

*'During the 1960s the average annual rate of (trade) increase (constant prices) was over 8%, while towards the end of the decade it accelerated to around 11%. Trade in manufactured goods increased almost twice as fast as trade in primary products (food, raw materials and fuels), so that by 1970 exports of manufactures accounted for two-thirds of total world trade. Throughout the decade, international trade increased substantially faster than world output . . . The share of world trade accounted for by the developed countries increased from 47% in 1960 to 55% in 1970.' David Robertson, 'The Enlarged EEC in the International Trading System, in *Britain in the EEC*, ed. Douglas Evans (Gollancz, 1973).

largest trade flows in 1970 were between the United States and the Nine future members of the enlarged EEC, and between the United States and Canada. Trade in invisibles, that is both investment income and services, has also grown steadily at an average annual rate of 10 per cent during the 1960s until it now accounts for more than a quarter of total world trade. An important factor in this growth in international trade and investment has been the growth in multinational companies and a consequent diminution in the significance of national frontiers. Among the major industrial countries the United States accounts for 60 per cent of total foreign investment — around $160 billion — with most of the remaining 40 per cent deriving from Western Europe and Japan. However, the influence of multinational companies cannot be limited to the amount of capital flowing from the parent company since in industrialised countries the greatest share of the capital is provided by local savings.

With eight of the world's ten largest multinational companies based in the United States it is no surprise that multinationals currently account for around 50 per cent of all U.S. exports. Significantly, the three top U.S. importers, by value, are Volkswagen, Datsun and Toyota, demonstrating the stimulation to trade in both directions which the multinational companies have until now provided among the industrialised countries. Since the policy options open to multinational companies are so much greater than those available to national companies the degree to which they can be regulated by national governments has steadily waned. Meanwhile, stimulated by the Kennedy Round of tariff cuts and despite the recent proliferation of non-tariff barriers, the economies of the industrialised countries have become increasingly integrated throughout the 1960s.

The Challenge of the 1970s

The challenge of the 1970s is not only to maintain and extend the level of integration which has brought undreamt prosperity to the industrialised countries, but to re-draw the world economic system in such a way as to enable the Third World to participate in the general prosperity. This means

including agriculture in the liberalisation of world trade. It
also means monitoring the activities of multinationals in the
developing world. Although only about one-third of the
activities of multinational companies are carried out in the
Third World their presence is relatively much more significant
in developing than developed countries, representing as they
often do a very high proportion of total investment capital,
technological knowhow and management skill. A recent
Report by the U.N. Department of Economic and Social
Affairs on Multinationals (1973) pointed out that the
developing economies account for much less than one-third
of the combined domestic product of developing and
developed countries confirming that the multinationals are
relatively more active in the Third World than elsewhere. The U.N. report revealed that among the developing
countries around 18 per cent of the total foreign direct
investment went to the Western hemisphere, 6 per cent to
Asia, 5 per cent to Africa, and 3 per cent to the Middle East.

The U.S. Diebold Institute predicts that during the next
twenty years European and Japanese multinationals will grow
faster than U.S. companies abroad on present trends.
Furthermore, that the labour migrations of the last twenty
years would be ended because of the social problems they
had created. In their stead, for instance, European manufac-
turers would establish their plant in Spain or North Africa to
take advantage of cheap and plentiful labour sources. This
prophecy tends to be confirmed by the German industrial
pattern where there are signs of the emergence of a future
pattern of German multinationals. This is partly a response to
the revaluation of the Deutsche mark but also to an
awareness that inflation, trade union militancy and labour
shortages have become semi-permanent features of the
German industrial scene. The combined results of these
factors have been to lessen the competitiveness of German
goods. Since exports comprise a third of turnover of many
West German companies and unit costs are the highest in
Western Europe, there is a growing awareness among
managers that German companies must expand their production abroad. Indeed, it has become government policy to
increase foreign investment spending. Among the big German

companies, AEG-Telefunken, BASF, Bayer, Daimler-Benz, Hoechst and Siemens all already have major foreign production operations while dozens more are investigating the prospects.

To illustrate the general drift of affairs, the expected expansion of German multinationals predicted by the Diebold Institute in Spain and North Africa is likely to be part of a general commercial expansion of the EEC on its southern fringes, mopping up cheap and plentiful labour. Such expansion is likely to hasten the admission of countries like Portugal, Spain and Greece into the Community. This commercial and subsequent political expansion of the EEC in the Mediterranean, spearheaded by the multinationals, is complemented by a long-term French diplomatic strategy to counterbalance the non-Latin northern tier of the EEC. It is my personal view that it is likely to be a much more powerful pull than any regional policy devised in Brussels to attract multinationals to Britain. But what of multinationals belonging to the other major Western superbloc — Japan?

Japan's growth pattern is coming under similar pressures to Germany with enforced revaluation of the yen, increasingly active trade unions and environmental problems arising from an extremely fast rate of industrialisation on an overcrowded archipelago. In Japan's case she is likely to expand chiefly in the Pacific and South-East Asia regions not only for their obvious proximity but also because they contain most of the needed raw materials. However, there are growing signs that Japan will make a major drive in the enlarged EEC market in the next few years and though she is unlikely to gain a major manufacturing base within the Community, like Germany she may well attempt to establish multinational operations in the Mediterranean countries. Even without such bases Datsun was the largest car importer into Britain in mid-1973. Against this background it is easy to understand that Japan, like the United States, has been concerned about EEC trade preferences with the Mediterranean countries (see Chapter 3 in detail), which provides one of the compelling reasons why Dr Kissinger has endeavoured to bring Japan into the scope of the new Atlantic dialogue between America and Europe. Once the major British and French companies begin to follow

West Germany's example by expanding their activities on the southern fringes of the EEC then the Community will extend its bounds if only to keep competitors like the Japanese and Americans firmly at bay.

So far the multinationals, judged by the admittedly scanty available evidence, have had a generally beneficial influence on balance on the industrialised world. To date they have behaved no better but also no worse than the majority of home-grown companies. However, as the superblocs develop and the number of multinationals multiplies competition between the multinationals is likely to intensify. The question is, will multinationals, under the pressure of events, be either turned or turn themselves into the advance guard of the expanding superbloc reinforcing the tendency towards regional economic exclusiveness? The tools are to hand. Certainly the European multinationals have always backed the enlargement of the EEC and contrary to popular opinion would generally prefer to deal with a single, favourably disposed EEC authority removed from many of the pressures of local and national accountability. Just as it would be foolish to categorise the multinationals as some intentionally malevolent influence so it would be equally foolish to ignore the common interests of the superblocs and its home-grown multinationals. If multinationals grow in size, numbers and influence, as seems most likely, the question arises to which political authority will they be accountable. At this point in time no ideal political authority exists. Should protectionism gain a hold then multinationals would be caught up squarely in the middle and would have little option presumably except to forge an alliance with their particular superbloc. There can be no doubt that it would be a case of both interacting upon the other and it would become harder than ever to determine which partner was originating major policy, or, put bluntly, who was wagging whom. Any general conclusion from such a brief survey would be out of place but one can register the suspicion that in the medium term multinationals are likely to accentuate the strains in a multipolar economic system and to heighten the chances of conflict.

The question arises does all this add up to any discernible pattern? That is a question which we can usefully postpone answering until the concluding section of this book. Meantime, in order to draw the threads of this chapter together, it may be helpful to enunciate a brief theory of economic multipolarity.

The Theory of Economic Multipolarity

As the mercantilist system of thought developed in the formative period of the emerging nation state so the recent growth of the new mercantilism has coincided with the emergence of the superbloc (outlined in this book) whose political power rests more on the combined gross product of its constituent states than their combined military capacity. However, in seeking to maximise the gross product of the superbloc that they command the political élite must justify their policies in terms of the interests of their component states and their citizens. One of the commonest forms of contemporary mercantilism practised by the superbloc is a belief in acquiring money by a balance of payments surplus by means of import substitution (e.g. the CAP which helped make the Six 90 per cent self-sufficient in agriculture) supported by a combined policy of import taxes and export subsidies. This has the effect of increasing the gross product but it can only logically do so at the expense of the other superblocs. The implicit danger contained in the apparently coincidental growth of the superbloc and protectionist policies — which in fact mutually feed on each other — is that they invite a fundamental conflict likely to harm not simply the superbloc at loggerheads but the entire world economic system.

The essence of the theory of economic multipolarity is therefore in summary as follows. The modern industrialised world has become heavily interdependent and rationally should become more interdependent. However, a small number of economic great powers (superblocs) have arisen. Though it is perfectly possible for these superblocs to co-exist and even to promote each other's economic prosperity they currently contain protectionist features which are bound to bring the superblocs into conflict. In the case of the enlarged EEC, the two major

protectionist features, the CAP and the Common External
Tariff, constitute the twin pillars of the Community which it
would be difficult to dismantle without the EEC ceasing to
be a superbloc. The inescapable conclusion is that the present
structure and tendencies, by accentuating the self-sufficient
character of the superblocs and reversing the trend towards
interdependence, contains the seeds of economic warfare.
Moreover, as outlined in this book, the five superblocs appear
likely to maintain the countries of Asia, Africa and Latin
America in an increasingly exclusive and in consequence
dependent relationship. As part of the superbloc's 'sphere of
expansion' the countries of the Third World would be drawn
into any conflict between the superpowers and be among the
first to suffer from its negative consequences. The Middle
East in particular represents an area where at least four of the
five superblocs come into conflict — the EEC and the Soviet
Union directly as they expand their general influence in the
area and the United States and Japan as they safeguard their
oil interests. And to add to this set of conflicting
interests between the superblocs there are America's indis-
soluble bonds with Israel, and the scale of Soviet military
support for the Arabs, and we are faced with a classic
confrontation between the world's two superpowers in-
volving economic and strategie interests combined with
national prestige on the grand scale. All these factors are
likely to aggravate an area where potentially each of the
world's superblocs has substantial conflicts of interest. None
of this evidence is to suggest that the trend towards
protectionism or the inclination towards conflict between the
superblocs is either inevitable or irresistible. It is one of the
objects of this book to show that both these forces exist and
to demonstrate the fact in some detail. Without much wider
recognition of the power and extent of these twin forces they
cannot be effectively checked or redirected. In the succeed-
ing chapters we will simply describe the nature of the
superblocs as they have already arisen whether in substance
or outline. By the end of the book, in the Conclusion, we will
be in a position to weigh the strength of these forces and the
possibilities for moderating them where possible.

3 The Evolution of Eurafrica

From the moment Britain joined the European Economic Community in January 1973, the consequences were bound to reach in time throughout the whole extent of sub-Saharan Africa. For the admission of Britain, with her close political and economic links with black African states containing more than 100 million people, opened up a wide range of possible relationships between black Africa and the enlarged EEC, which, not counting Britain, includes four ex-colonial powers in Africa, in France, Belgium, Italy and Germany. By the beginning of 1975, when the renegotiation of the Yaoundé and Arusha Conventions must be completed, the whole of Commonwealth Africa, including Nigeria, Ghana, Sierra Leone, Gambia, Zambia and Malawi, but excluding Kenya, Uganda and Tanzania (which are already associates), must make the basic decision whether they wish to take up the EEC Commission's offer of becoming associates or not. The type of association which they can choose from takes three distinct forms: (1) association under the Yaoundé|Convention; (2) association under terms similar to the Arusha model, or (3) a special bilateral trading agreement, confined to specific commodities, between the EEC and the African countries concerned.

The issues at stake are of crucial importance to the future development and welfare not only of the prospective associates of Commonwealth Africa but also to the twenty-one associates who already belong to the Yaoundé or Arusha groups. Clearly, the precise consequences of an expanded group of associated African states will only become apparent in the course of the Yaoundé and Arusha renegotiations. However, on the assumption that some idea of the future possibilities can be gleaned from the past, it is possible to

trace the history and development of both the Yaoundé and
Arusha groups, how they work, whom they have most
benefited, and where their members differ from the prospective Commonwealth African associates. Nor should we overlook the political consequences for the relations between
Francophone and Commonwealth Africa, and between independent black Africa and the rest of the continent.

From the earliest beginnings of the EEC — in the preamble
to the Rome Treaty, for instance — there is an acknowledge-
ment of the responsibilities of the Six to the less developed
world. However, it is framed significantly in terms of a
'resolve to confirm the solidarity which links Europe and the
countries overseas'. That is, it was always conceived in terms
of strengthening the ties which already existed between the
members of the Six and their former colonies (excepting
Luxembourg, which had none), of which the French and
Belgian colonies in Africa composed the most important part.
Moreover, from the beginning there was always a firm
distinction between those countries on the fringes of Europe,
such as Spain and Greece, which could become associates
with an expectation of eventual membership, and, on the
other hand, countries like those in Africa, which would
remain associates for as long as they wished but could never
expect admission as full members. This is an important
principle to bear in mind when we examine the extra-
ordinarily close economic ties between Europe and the
majority of black African states.

History of Yaoundé

The Yaoundé Convention was signed at Yaoundé, capital of
Cameroun, in July 1963, by representatives of the Six and
eighteen African states — Burundi, Central African Republic,
Cameroun, Chad, Congo (Brazzaville), Congo (Kinshasa), now
renamed Zaïre — Dahomey, Gabon, Ivory Coast, Madagascar,
Mali, Mauritania, Niger, Rwanda, Senegal, Somalia, Togo,
Upper Volta — which had formerly been linked with France,
Belgium and Italy. It came into force in June 1964. Its twin
principles were reciprocal free trade and financial aid from the
Six. The Convention grew out of the Rome Treaty on a highly

pragmatic basis during the latter half of the 1950s and early part of the 1960s. It was designed to suit widely differing requirements. On the one hand, the requirements of the Belgian Congo which had an 'open door' trade system; on the other, those African states linked with France which were generally highly protected and operated under generous French preferences. As these African states achieved their independence, only one, Guinea, chose to opt out of the preference system with the former colonial power.

In time, the Yaoundé Convention became the basic model for all non-European associates. The Arusha Convention between the Six and three East African states, Kenya, Uganda and Tanzania, was signed in September 1969. In this there were fare more limited concessions made on both sides, and, unlike the Yaoundé group, the Arusha countries do not qualify for any grants or loans from the European Development Fund. A second Yaoundé Convention came into force in January 1971 and is effective until January 1975. The renegotiation of this agreement will reveal the concrete terms available to the new prospective associates. In the meantime, it is essential to know how the two Conventions have worked so far.

How Yaoundé Operates

The Yaoundé Association agreement now embraces three main elements — reciprocal trade preferences, joint institutions and a multilateral aid fund. The trade arrangements between the Nine and their associates take the form of free trade treaties, not to be confused with trade agreements. The essential difference between the two is that a free trade treaty has very definite reciprocal rights and obligations. Thus, when the Nine grant import preferences to the associates, the associates are expected in turn to grant a measure of *reverse preferences* to imports from the Community. These reverse preferences have been the cause of considerable controversy and are highly significant in assessing the alternatives open to African states in the near future. The United States has consistently opposed the entire principle of reverse preferences and has stated that should it introduce a general preference scheme for the less developed countries, it would automatically exclude any developing country that continued to grant reverse preferences after 1975 (in effect after the expiry of the Yaoundé II Convention).

In spite of the fact that the actual value of reverse preferences granted by African countries is generally small, the principle is taken quite seriously. Thus the Arusha agreement, like that of Yaoundé, grants low, most favoured nation customs tariffs to EEC imports, and imposes high fiscal duties on imports from all other sources. There is not much doubt that these provisions are in contravention of the General Agreement on Trade and Tariffs (GATT) and the United Nations Conference on Trade and Development (UNCTAD) resolutions.

It may be argued that the extension of the reciprocity principle is justified on the grounds of protecting the original eighteen African signatory nations of the Yaounde Convention. With the exception of Zaïre, Ivory Coast and Senegal, they are all extremely poor countries. Indeed, the next round of negotiations will almost certainly be dominated by the Community's desire to protect (1) its own processed agricultural goods, and (2) the preferences of the original associates.

As a clear example, the Arusha agreement created tariff quotas for coffee, cloves and canned pineapples, all of which were likely to compete directly with the Yaoundé associates. Moreover, the four commodities — copper, timber, coffee and cocoa — which account for more than 50 per cent of Yaoundé exports to the Community at the present time are all major exports of the prospective Commonwealth African states, so the likelihood is that further and considerably stricter tariff quotas will be applied to match the number and size of the new associates.

It is generally agreed that the main value of the institutions of the Yaoundé and Arusha agreements is their betterment of EEC-Africa relations, and their contribution to the trend towards closer regional co-operation within Africa itself. The major body under both agreements is an Association Council composed of the members of the EEC Council of Ministers and a member of the government of each associated state. Although it meets only once a year, it has proved a good means of maintaining contact at the highest level; and it is empowered to take decisions binding on the associates. In addition, the Yaoundé and Arusha groups both maintain councils, committees and secretariats for co-ordinating their joint activities. Yaoundé also maintains an Associates Committee, a Parliamentary Conference and a Court of Arbitration — all three largely an inheritance from the French Community from which Yaoundé sprang.

The aid programme of the Yaoundé Association operates through the European Development Fund and the European Investment Bank. Two preliminary points are worth making. First, according to the Pearson Report, loans (which account for 50 per cent of bilateral aid to the less developed countries) are becoming increasingly swallowed up in repayment and interest charges. In Africa the servicing of loan debts takes 73 per cent of all new loans. Secondly, while aid accounts for something like 2 per cent of the value of all Third World exports to the developed countries, in Francophone Africa aid represents around 33 per cent of the value of their exports. Thus its relative importance to the Yaoundé group is much greater than for most other developing countries.

The principal reasons why the Yaoundé states receive so much aid are fourfold. They are among the poorest countries in the world (average income is less than 100 U.S. dollars per head), they possess few natural resources, several are landlocked and the majority are barely viable in strict economic terms. Although they represent only 4 per cent of the population of the Third World, they receive around 6 per cent of all aid to developing countries (some governments have complained that their civil servants' loyalty is greater to Paris than to the local national government). Against these revealing statistics it is easier to see why the politics of aid from the EEC has become such a central issue in the Yaoundé group.

The advantage of the European Development Fund is that 90 per cent of its aid is in the form of outright grants. Furthermore, its loans are long-term and at very low rates of interest. However, whereas the Yaoundé associates and dependencies receive around 40 per cent (compared with 50 per cent of all British aid disbursed to Commonwealth Africa), of all aid given by the member states of the EEC only 6 per cent of total EEC aid to the Third World was distributed through the Community's institutions. The majority of aid is either bilateral or disbursed through alternative multilateral institutions like the World Bank.

Britain has already agreed to contribute to the European Development Fund, beginning in 1975, but the size of the contribution will depend very much on the number of Commonwealth African states which decide to become associates. If Britain decided that its EDF contribution was to be *in addition* to its normal aid programmes, then this would improve the relative position of the associates. But if its contribution to the EDF was deducted from its overall aid programme, then those African states who choose to remain non-associates would be absolutely worse off.

Alternatively, if the British contribution to the EDF were to be deducted from bilateral aid to those countries which intended to become associates, there would be no fundamental alteration in British aid flows. What is clear is that Britain's decision on this matter, which will presumably only arise in the negotiations, will be of considerable importance in the calculations of Commonwealth African states.

What then can we conclude about the Yaoundé and Arusha agreements and their implications for possible new associates?

First, there seems to have been no spectacular *increase* in trade dependence on the EEC by the Yaoundé associates (though *aid* dependence is a different story). Exports from the Yaoundé group to the Community, for instance, have risen less on average than their exports to other countries. The same is true of imports. The explanation is partly that the majority of the Yaoundé states had already such close ties with France that further large percentage increases were most improbable. What has taken place, however, has been a fairly healthy degree of diversification of trade with France's partners in the original Community, most notably with Germany and Italy.

Yaoundé exports to the EEC have, in fact, fallen relative to other African states.* Partly this has been because the non-associate states of Africa are more economically developed, which suggests that they might be more competitive still if they became associates. This in turn argues for quota restraints to protect the original Yaoundé associates.

Secondly, the very fact that the Yaoundé states choose to readopt the second Yaoundé Convention suggests that it was, at least for them at that particular moment in history, the best available alternative. No more and no less than that can be read into the readoption decision.

Thirdly, the trade benefits for the Yaoundé association have been unequal to match their own unequal levels of economic development. If one had to name a single country which had benefited most in absolute terms from the Yaoundé Convention, it would unquestionably be France. France's exports to the Yaoundé Associates (which almost exactly match its imports) have grown during the 1960s by an amount greater in absolute terms than all its five partners put together. But this in itself is of far less importance to France than the fact that it imports more than one-third of total EEC imports from the Yaoundé group. Similarly, in spite of the fact that France gained around 40 per cent of the contracts under the EDF, this was relatively far less important to France than the aid the Yaoundé associates received under the Fund's auspices.

Fourthly, the Yaoundé and Arusha groups have consciously and successfully encouraged greater intra-African trade, notably in customs co-operation on a regional level in both West and East Africa. Should a large proportion of Commonwealth Africa opt for associate membership of the EEC in some form or another, there is a distinct possibility that it would unite in a practical manner the hitherto very much separated Francophone and Commonwealth Africa. It will be ironic if the very European states which 100 years ago divided the continent among themselves prove the means of unification in the post-colonial period.

*Between 1958 and 1971 the associated states' exports to the Community rose by an average of 6.2 per cent per annum compared with 7 per cent for the Third World as a whole.

Southern Africa*

The appointment in June 1971 of a South African
Ambassador to the EEC with the task of negotiating
exemptions for various South African exports highlights the
low-key but persistent attempt being made by the Republic
to preserve her privileged access to British markets following
entry. The indispensable role that Britain plays as both a
trading partner and as a source of investment for South
Africa is something that the Republic clearly wishes to carry
over to the enlarged Community. The extent to which the
British and South African economies have been linked in the
past has often been underplayed, but the central features of
the relationship are clear enough. Britain is at once both
South Africa's largest single external market (in 1970 it took
30 per cent of all South African exports) and by far the most
important source of foreign capital accounting for around 60
per cent of total foreign investment in South Africa. In turn
South Africa is the U.K.'s fifth largest single export market
after the United States, West Germany, the Irish Republic
and the Netherlands.

In 1968, the last year when complete figures were
available, the U.K. invested £600 million in South Africa or
around 10 per cent of all U.K. overseas investment making
her, after Australia, Canada and the United States, the fourth
most important destination for U.K. foreign investment.
Together these ties make Anglo-South African economic
relations of critical importance to both countries, but
especially to South Africa. Moreover, apart from the sterling
area, 25 per cent of South Africa's foreign capital comes from
Western Europe. Thus, in round terms, 80 per cent of South
Africa's outside investment derives from the enlarged EEC.
When you recall that 70 per cent of South Africa's direct
investment in 1970 came from abroad the importance of
EEC investment becomes even more apparent. In 1971, when
South Africa made a net capital gain from foreign investment
of £430 m, 30 per cent of the foreign capital went into
manufacturing and 25 per cent into mining. Total foreign
capital invested in South Africa is estimated at £3,400 m, of

---

*An article by the author entitled *Many Happy Returns From South Africa*,
based on this section, was published in *The Times* on 15 March, 1973.

which around £2,000 m comes from the sterling area. The
reasons for this massive flow of direct investment are not
hard to find. Apart from the fact that South Africa has never
nationalised a foreign company the rate of return on foreign
investments are, to put it mildly, extremely attractive.
Britain, for instance, is earning an average return of 12.1 per
cent on her South African investments compared with
returns of 8.9 per cent on her American investments, 6.6 per
cent on her Australian, 5.1 per cent on her Canadian and an
overall average of 8 per cent on all her foreign investments.
The United States has been even more fortunate in realising
as much as 19.3 per cent on her South African investments,
among the very highest from any of her foreign holdings.
That this fantastic performance in terms of both growth and
profitability is based on cheap, black labour, half of whom
are migrant workers semi-permanently separated from their
families, must also be recorded.

Another feature which the EEC and Southern Africa
(embracing South Africa, South-West Africa, the Bantustans,
Malawi, Zambia, Rhodesia, Angola and Mozambique, on
which the political economy of the Republic of South Africa
is predicated) share in common is a polarised pattern of
industrial development, which means that investment is
drawn to central growth areas while the outer regions are
neglected. The moral obligation to examine means of
restructuring both systems to make them accountable to
something besides purely market forces hardly need be
underlined. The available evidence suggests that the future
policies of the EEC, both in the public as well as the private
sector, are crucial to South Africa.

Meanwhile, in the trade field, South Africa's Minister of
Economics warned South Africans in 1970 that they stood to
lose 11 per cent of their exports following British entry. As
for Australia, the seriousness of such a threat lies not so
much in its total percentage of exports as in the manner in
which its effects are likely to be concentrated. Thus 45 per
cent of South Africa's exports to Britain including fresh and
canned fruit, wines and meat, which have previously been
admitted duty free, or at least at reduced tariffs, will now
have to pay increased rates under the EEC's Common
External Tariff. Remembering that in 1970 Britain bought

half South Africa's total exports of fresh deciduous and citrus fruit it is not difficult to foresee difficulties ahead for fruit growers. In the case of citrus fruits South Africa's success is due partly to a seasonal advantage over Australia and partly to her excellent marketing arrangements. But for many fruits South Africa's exports to Britain have flourished because of the protection of Commonwealth preference which South Africa retained by a special Act which was passed after she left the Commonwealth in 1961. For in spite of the temporary respite of a reduction of EEC tariffs on South African citrus fruits from 15 per cent to 5 per cent for a transitional period of two years nothing can disguise the fact that South Africa will have to face unequal competition as a supplier of the U.K. market, from France and Italy in particular, on a wide range of agricultural exports. Since Britain buys 75 per cent of South Africa's canned fruit and as the world's largest importer of canned fruit imports more than the whole of the rest of the Community, these are far from trifling issues.

With so much at stake South Africa has had to be content with haggling on a commodity by commodity basis, careful not to upset her overall relationship with a Community on whose goodwill her present pattern of industrial development depends. There are shoals ahead, however, in the coming year as the Community must choose between protecting the interests of some of the new prospective African associated states (especially in exports such as groundnuts and asbestos) and those of South Africa. One means open to South Africa will undoubtedly be to establish industries in African associated member states which would also tie in with her expanding economic strategy in the sub-continent. With combined EEC exports to South Africa worth about £650 m (including French armaments) South Africa is not without her own cards to play in the economic power game.

The Mediterranean

While France, Italy and Britain have each preserved traditional political and commercial ties with the Mediterranean countries, up until recently it was a haphazard and unco-ordinated affair. However, in 1972, the EEC Commission drew up a report (at the request of the Council of Ministers) which proposed a free trade area between the EEC and the Mediterranean countries to become fully effective by 1977. The report recommended that Spain, Portugal, Greece and Turkey be groomed for full membership on the assumption that they will in the future move towards more democratic government.

For several reasons the United States has severely criticised the Commission's proposals. First, not only does such a series of agreements run counter to attempts to liberalise world trade through GATT, but by insisting on reverse preferences it torpedoes any hope of developing a global development strategy for the underdeveloped countries. Secondly, and more immediately, if such agreements are made they will exclude U.S. exports from the Mediterranean. Third, such economic arrangements cannot be divorced from increased EEC political and military interest in the area. Far from accepting that the Mediterranean lies within an exclusive EEC sphere of influence, the U.S. maintains that the U.S. Sixth Fleet is the only credible counter to the ambitions of the Soviet Union in the area. Any third force, the U.S. maintains, will upset the delicate balance between the superpowers in the region. A fourth objection would be the non-democratic nature of the four proposed future members, Greece, Turkey, Spain and Portugal.

Seven Categories of Applicants

Meanwhile around fifteen countries of the Mediterranean area have already signed either association or trade agreements of some kind or have at the very least applied to do so. Since their circumstances and expectations vary considerably it is no surprise that these fifteen countries have reached around seven recognisably different forms of relationship with the EEC to date. First, there are Greece and Turkey, who signed association agreements in 1962 and 1964 respectively. Though they are both ruled by military regimes they are each unofficially moving towards full membership, Greece in 1984! Secondly, Spain and Portugal are two further prospective full members, both non-democratic, who currently have trade agreements with the EEC. Thirdly, there are the three Maghreb countries of Morocco, Algeria and Tunisia, who are each negotiating association arrangements at the moment. Fourthly, there are the Commonwealth islands of Cyprus (an applicant for association) and Malta (who already has a trade agreement with the EEC). Fifthly, there are the three Arab states of Lebanon, Egypt and Jordan, together with Iran, all of whom are applicants for some form of arrangement, with Egypt wishing to extend her trade agreement into association. Sixthly, there is Yugoslavia, who also has a trade agreement which she hopes to expand. Seventhly, and lastly, there is Israel, who has a trade treaty which she wishes to renegotiate and transform into a form of association. Taken together, it is apparent that these very individual arrangements grew out of varying requirements at differing stages. Any attempt to standardise relations between the EEC and these fifteen countries must manifestly have profound political-strategic consequences. Here, however, we will concern ourselves with the economic factors which underlie the network of changes threatening to take place.

The Current Associates

Officially, ever since the military takeover in Greece (population nine million) in April 1967, the association agreement has been suspended until the restoration of parliamentary democracy. In practice, both Greece and the EEC proceed as if full membership was inevitable. Thus, as in Britain, Value Added Tax (VAT) was introduced in 1973 as required by the association agreement. Since Germany is already Greece's largest export market and the U.K., Italy and France are her third, fourth and fifth largest foreign suppliers respectively, the economic links already exist. Greece, however, relies considerably on invisible earnings from tourism (which doubled from 1966 to 1971), from emigrant remittances and from merchant shipping, in all three of which the U.S. makes a substantial financial contribution. More directly, President Nixon's decision in

March 1972 to override the U.S. Congress's decision to cut off military aid to Greece and the further decision of his Administration to base part of the U.S. Sixth Fleet on Piraeus (the port of Athens), lent invaluable support to Greece's foreign exchange earnings.

Turkey, the only other current EEC associate member besides Greece, has around four times the population (population 36 million) of whom 70 per cent are engaged in agriculture, which provides 90 per cent of Turkey's export earnings (cotton alone earns 30 per cent). In 1972 unemployment reached the two million mark (around 14 per cent of the labour force), without counting considerable rural underemployment. As in many Middle East countries where the officer class represent the spearhead of reform, the Turkish army has been seeking to introduce further land reforms but has so far been blocked by the majority party in parliament. Meanwhile around 40 per cent of all Turkish exports go to Common Market countries (compared with 10 per cent to the U.S.), of which Germany absorbs half. After Germany and the U.S., Italy, Britain, Switzerland and France are Turkey's next most important markets. The general trade pattern would suggest an increasingly close relationship with the EEC culminating in full membership. U.S. exports to Turkey (running at around $13 million) would certainly be adversely affected.

The Potential Members

In June 1970 Spain signed a preferential trade agreement with the EEC. This included arrangements for the EEC to remove its tariffs on Spanish industrial goods by 60 per cent by the end of 1973. In return Spain agreed to reduce her tariffs on EEC exports by between 25 per cent and 60 per cent over a period of six years. Spain's chief immediate concern following the enlargement of the Community is the threatened loss of entry of Spanish fruit and vegetables, which have been traditionally exported to Britain. Spain is thus seeking a renegotiation. Meanwhile the EEC Commission wants a more democratised system of government before full membership is contemplated, though President Pompidou has made no secret of his wish to admit Spain and Portugal at the earliest possible date.

Although Portugal remains a member of EFTA she concluded a trade agreement with the EEC in July 1972 providing for mutual reductions in industrial tariffs (from 1 April 1973 to 1 July 1977). In recent years Portugal has suffered from a labour shortage as up to 100,000 Portuguese citizens emigrate annually to work in the countries of the enlarged EEC, a figure which could increase if local wages rise too rapidly and foreign investors move elsewhere. Some idea of the dependence of Portugal on EFTA in the last few years can be seen in the fact that in 1971 EFTA members bought 40 per cent of Portuguese exports (chiefly pearls, wine, cork and fish) and supplied around 25 per cent of her imports (mainly foodstuffs and machinery). Among her former EFTA partners Britain was by far the most important, accounting for nearly 30 per cent of Portugal's total exports and around 15 per cent of her imports. The three largest sources of investment capital in 1971 were South Africa (largely in Mozambique), Britain and the U.S., of which South Africa provided exactly double that of Britain. The U.S. currently accounts for around 10 per cent of total Portuguese exports the enlarged EEC about 50 per cent. Under the latest EEC trade agreement Portugal's exports are likely to switch increasingly towards the EEC, hastening the day of full EEC membership. Britain's entry accentuates this trend.

The Maghreb Bloc

In 1964 the member states of the Maghreb, Morocco, Algeria and Tunisia, were linked together in the Maghreb Permanent Consultative Committee, but differences of approach over economic development and especially foreign investment have hindered any really close economic co-operation. Although closely linked with France in the past, Algeria, the largest of the three, has registered a switch in her foreign trade away from France and towards Britain, Spain, Japan and the U.S. Two factors in this trend have been Algeria's with to gain control of the key sectors of her industry, notably oil (which invited reprisals by France, reduced exports and eventually forced import controls on Algeria) and the difficulty of gaining entry into the EEC for Algerian wine. The latter item especially has been a major stumbling-block in the attempts made so far to draw up a treaty of association between the EEC and Algeria. For while Algeria's mineral and industrial sectors have promising futures her agricultural sector is extremely vulnerable. Meanwhile, the Algerians have negotiated major sales of natural gas to the U.S. over the next twenty-five years as well as with West Germany, France, Belgium and Spain. Tunisia, whose trade deficit is balanced by earnings from invisibles such as tourism, overseas workers' remittances and capital inflows, is, like Algeria, closely linked with the EEC and especially with France, who takes 20 per cent of Tunisian exports. Tunisia's tourist industry, helped along with loans from the World Bank, is the fastest growing sector of her economy.Morocco, also an agricultural country (70 per cent of the labour force and 50 per cent of all exports come from off the land), relies on tourism, remittances from Moroccans abroad and outside capital investment to produce a payments surplus. Morocco's closest trading links are with Spain but like both her neighbours to the east she hopes to obtain an enlarged trading agreement with the EEC, that is, improved terms of association.

The Arab Middle East Bloc

In 1971 more than 60 per cent of all Egyptian exports (principally cotton) went to the East European countries and only 12 per cent to Western Europe. The Soviet Union took 42 per cent of Egypt's total exports in 1971. Since then there has been a significant decline in Egypt—Soviet relations which has encouraged Egypt to seek associate membership of the EEC with considerable encouragement behind the diplomatic scenes from France. Although Egypt's proposed merger with Libya could strengthen Egypt's financial and economic position very substantially, she will still need a major non-Arab trading partner for the foreseeable future. France plainly intends that it should be the enlarged EEC. Lebanon, Jordan and Iran, like Egypt, have also each sought association or trade agreements. Of these only Lebanon, again with strong French diplomatic support, has so far achieved substantial concessions, which include reductions on almost 60 per cent of Lebanese exports to the EEC. Britain, as Lebanon's second largest supplier (after France), will help to enlarge these arrangements. However, Lebanon's chief export market remains the other Arab countries, most notably Saudi Arabia and Kuwait, who also constitute a major source of investment.

The Mediterranean Commonwealth

Both the former British colonies in the Mediterranean are very keen, with British backing, to obtain associate membership with preferential arrangements for certain vital exports, for a time at least. In the past, 70 per cent of Cyprus' agricultural exports (around 60 per cent of her total exports are agricultural goods) have gone to Britain, which absorbs 40 per cent of the island's total exports. By comparison the Six took only 20 per cent of all Cypriot exports, almost all of it going to West Germany. Now Cypriot negotiators, who have sought to obtain an association agreement, are requesting concessions on grapes, citrus fruits and potatoes. So far, because of the dispute over the timing of the concessions and because of the EEC's desire to protect French and Italian grape growers, the Cypriots are far from happy. In particular, the Cypriots are seeking to gain a five-year transitional period for Cyprus sherry, which alone represents 10 per cent of her agricultural exports.

Meanwhile Malta already has a preferential trade agreement, but like Cyprus is heavily dependent on the British market. For despite diversification Britain still accounts for around 40 per cent of Malta's exports, chiefly clothing, machinery and rubber goods. Potatoes and onions, traditional Maltese exports, are likely to be effectively excluded from EEC markets.

Yugoslavia

The latest EEC–Yugoslav trade agreement which came into force in May 1973 covers about 37 per cent of total Yugoslav exports and 44 per cent of total Yugoslav imports. Its importance to Yugoslavia thus cannot be overestimated.

Yugoslavia's pre-eminent concerns have been twofold. First, to obtain less restricted entry for her exports of live cattle, pork, bacon, fruit preserves, tobacco, wine and fish. Secondly, to obtain transit rights for Yugoslav ports to enable them to handle goods such as citrus fruits and maize imported into the EEC. Up until now maize coming through Italian ports, for instance, has been more favourably treated than that coming through Yugoslav ports. While Yugoslavia has developed strong commercial ties with both Italy and Germany (notably through Fiat and Volkswagen), the Soviet Union remains Yugoslavia's major export market, mainly in minerals.

Israel

Although, failing membership, Israel would like to obtain associate status, for the moment she has had to be content with renegotiating in 1972 her preferential trade agreement (the original agreement was signed in July 1970), with strong support from the Netherlands and Germany. As France has so far backed the Arab interest, Israel hopes that in the enlarged Community Britain will champion the Israeli interest. This is important when considering the main economic disadvantages to Israel. These lie chiefly in the threat to Israeli exports of oranges and citrus products to Britain and in the discriminatory EEC preferences given to oranges exported from the Maghreb countries.

A clear conflict between Israeli and Arab commercial interests may become increasingly apparent as the Community expands its links with the Mediterranean area countries. To complicate the issue even further, and bring the Middle East right into the middle of the U.S.—EEC dispute over monetary, defence and balance of payments questions, there is the current world shortage of oil. As the United States, notwithstanding the escalation in costs, becomes ever more reliant on Middle East oil, the chances of conflict over energy between the U.S., Japan and the EEC no longer seems a remote possibility. Moreover, the Middle East oil states, with their colossal financial reserves, could become a crucial factor in the bargaining preceding the reform of the world monetary system. That there will be some tough bargaining between the United States and the EEC (especially France) on the Mediterranean there can be little doubt.

Scandinavia

Norway's decision to stay out of and Denmark's to join the enlarged EEC leave wide open the future development of the north-eastern extremity of Western Europe. In particular, it leaves unanswered the question whether the proposed Nordic Economic Union (Nordec) between Norway, Sweden and Finland (and, originally, Denmark) may yet come to fruition — or, alternatively, whether Norway and Sweden will eventually join Denmark in the EEC. While there are undeniable strategic implications in the possible creation of a neutrally orientated Nordec, it is as well as to remember that at the moment Norway remains a loyal member of NATO, whereas France long since withdrew without any suggestion that she might become a neutral nation.

Denmark's decision to join the EEC is more or less on a par with Ireland's. Economically, both had too much to lose to make any other decision. It has been estimated that entry into the Common Market will benefit Denmark's balance of payments by around £35 million in the first year alone, rising to about £75 million in 1978. Conversely, if Denmark had stayed out it would have cost around £125 million annually (out of an annual export income of around £1,200 million) through the loss of existing agricultural markets (a 50 per cent stake of the British bacon market, for instance). The key factor in the clear economic advantage to Denmark accruing from EEC entry will be the opening up of a greatly expanded (and protected) market with guaranteed high prices. This should eventually stimulate substantial reinvestment in Danish agriculture. Unlike the remainder of the Nordic countries, Denmark's trade with Britain has remained relatively steady over the last three or four years. Following entry, both the quotas on her exports to Britain and the levies on her exports to the original Six were removed. The circumstances of the other Nordic countries vary considerably.

It was widely assumed before Britain's entry that Norway's decision to stay out of the EEC would have severely negative economic consequences. Yet even allowing that Norway failed to negotiate an especially favourable industrial free trade agreement with the EEC the picture is not entirely bleak. Norway's exports to Britain stood, in 1971, at 17.9 per cent of all Norwegian exports. Though this represented the largest single national export market, it was only 1.7 per cent ahead of Sweden. Furthermore, Norwegian exports to Britain have declined by about 20 per cent in the last three years. While Britain, Sweden and West Germany account for 40 per cent of all Norwegian exports (and imports), the most striking percentage growth in Norwegian exports has been with Nordic countries.

During the 1960s, Sweden, Denmark and Finland assumed as much importance as trade partners for Norway as the original Six members of the EEC. In the mid-1950s they took 17.6 per cent of Norway's exports and provided 14.5 per cent of her imports. By 1968 they purchased 24 per cent of Norwegian exports and accounted for 27 per cent of Norwegian imports. Although in the years between 1958 and 1968 Norway's trade with the EEC declined as a percentage of her total trade, more recently Norway's exports to the EEC have grown to about 30 per cent (mostly to Germany and the Netherlands).

For some time, more than 75 per cent of Norwegian exports to the EEC have been composed of aluminium and ferro-alloys, forest products and fish products, of which almost 50 per cent have had to face quota restrictions. Moreover, most of these exports were excluded from the Kennedy Round tariff cuts. Taken together, these factors led to unfavourable Norwegian public opinion and the EEC's failure to make any major concessions in the negotiations confirmed this attitude. But there were concrete economic disadvantages to entry too. These included the fact that Norway's guaranteed farm prices are generally higher than those of the Six and entry would have meant a fall of up to a third in farm incomes (Norway's farmers in the northern two-thirds of the country are subsidised to retain them on the land for both social and strategic reasons). Hence Norway's farmers, like her fishermen, almost unanimously opposed entry.

But what will happen now? Because Norway's foreign trade is so crucial to her economy (imports amount to 45 per cent of its GNP, exports to 40 per cent) and because 75 per cent of her exports (and 70 per cent of her imports) have in the past gone to either the European Free Trade Association (EFTA) or the EEC, Norway remains extremely sensitive to trading conditions in Europe. The industrial free trade agreement which Norway signed with the EEC in May 1973 goes some way to taking account of this vulnerability by providing for the progressive dismantling of tariffs on the majority of industrial goods by 1978, bringing Norway in line with Sweden in her relations with the EEC. Unlike Sweden, however, Norway remains very dependent on fish and farm producers. Moreover, Britain has been obliged under the EEC rules to impose tariffs on Norwegian paper products and frozen fish.

Having decided to stay outside the EEC, Norway seems likely to be drawn into closer association with her Nordic neighbours, Sweden and Finland. Taken together, they form not only Norway's most important trading partner (accounting for 19 per cent of Norwegian exports) but also her closest neighbours — physically, culturally and politically. The EEC's unwillingness to make greater concessions on aluminium (Norway's largest export earner), paper and ferro-alloys in the industrial free trade treaty with Norway could hasten the creation of a three-nation Nordic union of Norway, Sweden and Finland.

Neither Sweden, because of her political neutrality, nor Finland, because of her buffer-state status between the Soviet Union and NATO, have ever been serious candidates for EEC membership. The fact that Switzerland, Finland and Austria could all be members of EFTA illustrates the great difference between that association and the demands it makes, and the EEC. With eight million people, Sweden has twice the population of Norway (Finland has five million) and is an altogether far more industrialised and self-sufficient economy. Nevertheless, like Norway and Finland, she would stand to benefit from closer Nordic economic links. Indeed, even before the Norwegian and Danish referenda, it was no secret that Sweden wished them both to stay out.

At this point, Sweden, Finland and Norway have each negotiated industrial free trade agreements with the EEC. While these maintain free trade among the surviving members of EFTA and abolish intra-EEC/EFTA tariffs on the majority of industrial goods over the next four to five years, the EEC will only reduce tariffs on what it deems 'sensitive' products, such as paper and pulp, over a period extending until 1984. After 1977 Britain, too, will adopt the same time-table. Partly in anticipation of British entry, there has been a spectacular decline over the last three years in both Swedish and Finnish exports to Britain (60 per cent and 50 per cent respectively). For Finland, EEC enlargement is likely to increase trade with both Sweden and the Soviet Union, and possibly other East European countries. At the moment, Finland's major export markets are Britain (19 per cent), Sweden (16 per cent), the Soviet Union (11 per cent) and West Germany (10 per cent), which does not bear out the impression that Finland exists wholly in pawn to the Soviet Union.

More than 70 per cent of Sweden's external trade is currently carried out with members of the enlarged Community of Nine. Sweden is therefore most anxious to improve arrangements with the EEC, especially for paper and pulp (which still account for 15 per cent of her total exports) and to soften the tariffs which Britain and Denmark are obliged, as EEC members, to erect against Sweden. However, if Sweden is unable to negotiate more liberal arrangements with the EEC, she might well reactivate the proposals for Nordic economic union between herself, Norway and Finland. As the largest and most prosperous of the three, the initiative lies very much in Sweden's hands. A Nordic bloc could take advantage of the Soviet Union's increased trade with Western Europe but the likelihood is that it would develop closer links with the West European bloc. Its aim no doubt would be to steer an independent course.

4 The Soviet Union as a Eurasian Power

While world attention was concentrated on the summit detente diplomacy in 1972 between the United States and China and between the United States and the Soviet Union, the latter has also been drawing closer commercially, if less spectacularly, to the European Economic Community. Not only did Soviet foreign trade increase as a whole by more than 10 per cent in 1972 but it became increasingly diversified. Nowhere was this more striking than with the countries of Western Europe. Indeed between 1965 and 1972 the volume of trade between the Soviet Union and the countries of Western Europe more than doubled, increasing from 2,000 million roubles to 4,100 million roubles. Behind this striking growth in Soviet foreign trade is an almost entirely new element in Soviet policy. That element is the belief that foreign economic relations can play a significant role in raising the level of efficiency of the Soviet national economy. This view was made explicit by Leonid Brezhnev to the Twenty-fourth Party Congress in 1971. The Congress went on to set a growth target in foreign trade of between 33 and 35 per cent for the present Five Year Plan. This means a target of 30,000 million roubles by 1975. In 1972 it had already reached 26,000 million roubles.

As an indirect outcome of the new policy of utilising foreign trade as a spur to Soviet efficiency the Communist Party announced in April 1973 a draconian reorganisation of industry. In essence the changes involved the transfer of responsibility for management from central ministries to new associations of producers whose duties include the development of products for export. In the past, many Western businessmen complained that while it had the technological skills and capacities the Soviet Union was simply not producing goods saleable in the West. Since the present plan (1971—75) is seriously behind schedule it will be interesting to see if these changes make for any overall improvement. On the one hand there remains a general awareness by Soviet leaders that central planning is highly effective in mobilising and concentrating resources in time of war or pressing social deprivation. But on the other hand there is a feeling that modern industrial society has too many separate objectives for this to be the only road to Socialism. The twin facts remain that the majority of foreign trade is still conducted on the basis of long-term trade and economic agreements and that most of it is conducted with other Communist countries in Eastern Europe.

East European—Soviet Trade

Soviet trade with 'fellow socialist' countries amounted in 1972 to 16,800 million roubles (compared with 9,200 million roubles with non-Communist countries) which was a dramatic 70 per cent increase on 1965. This means that Eastern Europe accounts for more than 65 per cent of Soviet foreign trade. The expectation under the present plan (1971—75) is that Soviet trade with Eastern Europe will grow by around 50 per cent. By far the most important Soviet trading partner in Eastern Europe is East Germany, followed by Poland, Czechoslovakia, Bulgaria, Hungary and Romania. These close trade ties are further reinforced by close collaboration in a wide variety of scientific and technological projects between member states of the Council for Mutual Economic Assistance (COMECON).

The most important commodity sector in trade between the Soviet Union and the Communist countries of Eastern Europe is that in engineering products. In 1972 the Soviet Union imported 3,400 million roubles worth of engineering goods from COMECON member states which constituted very nearly half their total engineering exports. Such large-scale arrangements in industrial goods clearly make sense between centrally planned economies, not least because they can make their five- and even ten-year plans dovetail. Thus mammoth engineering imports into the Soviet Union have hastened the expansion of several Soviet industries, notably chemicals, metals, timber and food processing in addition to the Soviet merchant fleet and railway system. For her part the Soviet Union has been exporting increasingly large quantities of machinery and equipment to Eastern Europe and beyond. During the last five years machinery and equipment exports have increased by 70 per cent until they now represent nearly a quarter of all Soviet exports. The export of fuels, industrial raw materials and semi-manu-factured goods has also expanded by almost 45 per cent over the same period. In both these sectors Eastern Europe is by far the most important market. Thus the Soviet Union meets all COMECON countries' import requirements for oil and pig-iron, 90 per cent of their iron-ore import requirements, 80 per cent in sawn timber, 75 per cent in rolled metal and phosphorous fertilisers and 60 per cent in hard coal, manganese ore and cotton. Taking Soviet foreign trade as a whole, it is possible to say that in spite of the overall expansion with Western Europe, the United States and Japan the Soviet economy has never before been so closely linked with Eastern Europe than it is today.

West European–Soviet Trade

The degree of economic interdependence between the Soviet Union and the COMECON countries of Eastern Europe is currently considerably greater than that existing between the nine members of the EEC. This is salutary to remember when some commentators talk loosely of wooing members of the COMECON away from the Soviet Union and into the ambit of the EEC. This does not mean that the economic links between the two halves of Europe are not multiplying, merely that the Soviet Union is very much part of that coming together as the following figures demonstrate.

First, whereas Eastern Europe accounts for 65 per cent of Soviet foreign trade, Western Europe represents 15 per cent of total Soviet foreign trade. Thus, within the context of this world-wide trend towards competing trading blocs based on well-defined geographical boundaries, the Soviet Union, with 80 per cent of her foreign trade conducted with European countries, is no exception. In 1972 the Soviet Union's five major trading partners in Western Europe were West Germany (828 million roubles), Finland (606 million roubles), Britain (558 million roubles), France (554 million roubles) and Italy (466 million roubles). Among the big five, Soviet trade expansion with France recorded a spectacular increase of 170 per cent between 1965 and 1972. As with the other major West European trade partners, much of this trade growth has been assiduously fostered by a permanent Soviet–French commission for economic, scientific and technical co-operation. By the spring of 1973 Britain too had begun to draw up the outlines of a ten-year agreement on technical and industrial co-operation with the Soviet Union. Meanwhile the extension of commercial co-operation was one of the major items on the agenda of the all-European Conference on Security and Co-operation which itself reflects the current attempt to forge a European consciousness extending from the Atlantic to the Urals.

U.S.–Soviet Trade

No examination of the new economic patterns in Europe would be complete without a brief description of the newly transformed relationship between the United States and the Soviet Union. In terms of industrial capacity in Europe, the United States, with a current industrial stake in Western Europe estimated at $30 billion, is the pre-eminent industrial power. Thus, any alteration in the relationship between the Soviet Union (as we have seen, equally pre-eminent in Eastern Europe) and the United States is bound to have consequences for European industrial and commercial patterns, if not today then at least tomorrow. The most significant alteration in U.S.–Soviet trade relations took place with the signing of the U.S.–U.S.S.R. Trade Agreement in October 1972.

After twenty-eight years of mutual mistrust U.S.–Soviet commercial relations were pointed in the direction of the restoration of most favoured nation treatment, which had ceased to apply twenty years ago. The way was cleared for the agreement when the Soviet Union agreed to repay her lend-lease debts amounting to 722 million dollars over a period of years extending not later that 2001. In response, the United States removed most of the discriminatory tariffs against the Soviet Union. In effect the agreement guaranteed a tripling of U.S.–Soviet trade over a three-year period to about $1.5 billion. Since the agreement was between the governments of the two greatest military and economic powers on earth it needed to embrace a very strong measure of reciprocity. From the United States' point of view a balance of jobs surplus was no less important than its contribution to the U.S. balance of payments. Thus the agreement*provides that in return for Soviet imports of industrial raw materials and energy the United States will export increasing quantities of machine tools, earth-moving equipment, grain products and consumer goods. The significance of this for the 'European economy' is that these are the very exports that the United States has traditionally sent to Western Europe. The possibility arises that by guaranteeing a large market for U.S. machinery over an extended period the Soviet Union will strengthen the United States' competitive position in Western Europe. For the moment despite the provisions of the Treaty of Rome for a common commercial policy the nine members of the EEC make their own bilateral arrangements with Moscow, which leaves the United States unchallenged as the richest market with which the soviet Union can deal on a government to government basis. There is also the fact that the two superpowers have taken their first halting steps in the direction of complementary economics. This will mean they will both have vested interests in maintaining and expanding extra-European trade, which is a bonus at a time of trade blocs with exclusivist tendencies. This also applies with Soviet–Japanese trade, which in 1972 was valued at 800 million roubles. Much of the recent co-operation between the two countries has

---

*At the time this book went to press the U.S. Trade Reform Bill, which would have put the 1972 agreement into effect, was being seriously threatened as the House of Representatives inserted two amendments denying the Soviet Unions 'most favoured notion' treatment and business credits unless it allowed freedom of emigration. Although designed to allow the emigration of Soviet Jews to Israel, the Bill, as it stands, would apply equally to all Soviet citizens. If accepted by the Soviet Union it would represent a dramatic policy switch.

hinged around the provision of Japanese equipment to expand the pulp and paper industries in the Soviet Far East. Which brings us to the future of continental Asia.

The Asian Commonwealth

Ever since the Santiago conference of UNCTAD (United Nations Conference on Trade and Development), both Britain and the EEC have been made aware of the fears of the developing countries that the world is dividing up into great political and economic blocs from which the less developed countries will emerge in an ever more dependent position.

Just as former African colonies of Britain and France look like being linked to an enlarged EEC, so the Latin American states will probably be offered preferential arrangements by the United States. Assuming that neither the enlarged EEC nor the United States makes provision for them, this would leave Commonwealth Asia unattached. Unless the much discussed Pacific Free Trade Association (PAFTA) bloc (containing the United States, Canada, Japan, Australia and New Zealand at its core) develops rapidly and makes provision for Commonwealth Asian countries, the likelihood must be that by the end of the decade, if not before, much of Commonwealth Asia will fall under the Soviet sphere of influence, or that of China in the case of Pakistan (which has already left the Commonwealth). This would complete a series of three major North–South blocs in Asia – namely the Soviet Union, Japan and China and their respective economic satrapies – with the southern elements in these alliances in a permanently dependent relationship.

These are the overall political and economic alignments in Asia which seem likely to be hastened by the enlargement of the EEC, if only as defensive arrangements against a steady growth in protectionism. The economic effects of the enlargement of the EEC on Asia, and especially Commonwealth Asia, are likely to be even more acute in the short term.

The essential starting point for any understanding of the consequences of the enlargement of the EEC is that the

relationship between the Nine and the less developed
countries is crucial to the welfare of the latter. In 1970, for
instance, 30 per cent ($2,013 million) of all net official
development assistance from the Development Assistance
Committee (DAC) of the Organisation for Economic Co-
operation and Development (OECD), representing the
developed countries, derived from the Six, and 37 per cent
from the Nine. More important, the Nine have in the past
accounted for 40 per cent of the total exports of the less
developed countries. Thus the pattern of trade which the
enlarged EEC (which will be the largest component in the
world trading system) adopts is of fundamental importance
to the entire Third World.

Taking as a starting-point the fact that Britain must adjust
its trading pattern with the Third World to that of the EEC,
and not vice versa – a fact repeatedly stated by the Commission – the auspices for the developing countries are not
encouraging. At a stark and somewhat oversimplified level,
roughly 20 per cent of the total imports of the Six come
from less developed countries compared with Britain's 26 per
cent from the same source. A difference of 6 per cent seems
small enough. But if Britain's trade with the less developed
countries adapts to that of the Community, it would involve
a fall in imports from the developing countries of around $1
billion.

One mitigating factor is that the percentage of total trade
of the developing countries with the EEC has grown during
the last few years, while the percentage of their total trade
with Britain has declined. Nevertheless, since Britain, which
in general has provided better terms of trade to the
developing countries (most notably through her Commonwealth Preferences), is obliged to adapt to the EEC, whose
avowed aim remains one of self-sufficiency in agricultural
products, the effect is bound to be negative.

The fundamental reason for this negative effect is to be
found in the EEC's Common Agricultural Policy. For, just as
the CAP represents the major source of direct economic loss
for Britain arising from membership of the EEC (the CAP
accounted for 80 per cent of the total EEC budget, i.e.
approx. £2,000 m in 1973), so it also represents the major

source of loss to Commonwealth countries arising from British membership. Though the rest of this chapter is chiefly concerned with who will gain or lose what preferences, the central question in determining the trading pattern between an enlarged EEC and the developing countries is whether self-sufficiency will prevail or not against cheap foreign imports.

A major factor which must be borne in mind about the CAP is that its consequences are likely to become *increasingly* negative. This is true not only for the British taxpayer and consumer, who will constitute a new spur to production and a brake on coming to grips with reform by shouldering a disproportionate share of the cost, since Britain is a net importer of most foods, but also for the less developed countries. The basic reason is that while the 'green revolution' has opened up the prospect of the less developed countries becoming significant exporters of both rice and grains at highly competitive prices, the CAP specifically protects these products by a series of variable levies and quotas which effectively exclude regular supplies of cheap imports while maintaining high prices for the domestic product. Italy, for instance, has already dumped rice on the world market.

According to FAO (Food and Agriculture Organisation) estimates, approximately 50 per cent of all agricultural exports from the less developed countries compete against protected agricultural goods in the markets of the developed countries. Britain's entry into the EEC will substantially increase this percentage. Already, thanks to the protectionism of the developed countries, the share of the less developed countries in international trade in primary and processed agricultural goods — especially wheat, sugar, oils and fats — is falling faster than any other group of commodities. At the present rate, the enlarged EEC will shortly be supplying over half of its food requirements by internal trade as it moves steadily towards self-sufficiency in almost every food product. This then is the bleak general picture of EEC trade with the less developed countries of Commonwealth Asia who constitute by far the largest numerical group in population terms.

In 1970 the total value of exports by Asian Commonwealth countries to the U.K. was \$925 m which included \$327 m in processed agricultural goods and \$189 m in manufactured goods. When Britain joined the EEC she was essentially switching from an open system (cotton textiles being the only notable exception in Commonwealth Asian exports) to a quota system with tariffs on 'sensitive' products – i.e. domestic products vulnerable to competition. The major disadvantages for the Asian Commonwealth countries are, first, that processed agricultural goods and tropical products (e.g. cotton textiles, jute, coconut products, oilseeds, sugar and rice) will have to face either quotas or tariffs and, secondly, that the manufacturers of Hong Kong and Singapore will suffer considerable discrimination. At the moment a variety of ad hoc bilateral agreements between the EEC Commission and Asian Commonwealth countries like India and Bangladesh have arisen but they tend to hide the reality of restrictions by making 'voluntary' quota arrangements.

It is not the individual arrangements on certain products but the overall pattern of trade between the enlarged EEC and the Asian Commonwealth which must concern us. For the notable feature of the EEC's relationship towards the whole of Asia is the complete absence of any development strategy. Indeed, a special term has grown up to cover Asian (and for that matter Latin American) countries in EEC jargon, the 'non-associables' – sometimes called more bitterly the 'untouchables'. Underlying this division is the concept evolved by the Community that the EEC can only extend Association to relatively homogeneous geographical areas (e.g. the Yaoundé bloc of Francophone states in Africa), which of course makes it difficult for Britain to bring in her heterogeneous Commonwealth partners.

In summary, then, the general consequences of EEC enlargement for India, Pakistan, Ceylon, Bangladesh, Malaysia and Singapore include a loss of Commonwealth preferences in the U.K. market, discrimination by duty-free treatment of the Nine to each other, and discrimination by the special privileges accorded to the regional associates of the EEC, chiefly in Africa and the Mediterranean area. The policy which the EEC claims to cover the ill-effects of enlargement, the Generalised Scheme of Preferences (GSP), would be meaningful only if this scheme were acceptable to all industrialised countries, which it is not – and especially not to the United States. Furthermore, the GSP, as pointed out earlier, does not remove either the quotas for selected 'sensitive' products or the CAP's levies on major agricultural exports of the future, such as rice and grain. At first India and Pakistan negotiated special trading agreements with the EEC in specific products (like jute, coir, handicrafts and cotton textiles), later they managed to obtain general trade agreements. Both failed to extract any major concessions where such agreements might have conflicted with the CAP.

What general conclusions can be drawn? The trend of the enlarged EEC's trade policies seems fundamentally protectionist. Unless Britain can arrest this trend, which seems unlikely bearing in mind the entrenched nature of the CAP, the Asian Commonwealth might be best advised to lobby in Moscow. For it is in Moscow that the political will exists to make the sort of arrangements for guaranteed markets that the Commonwealth Asian countries so desperately need. In the case of Pakistan, Peking rather than Moscow holds the key. The entry of Britain into the EEC marks the end of British economic influence not only in India but most of South Asia. As we shall see in two later chapters there are three new great powers in the ascendancy in Asia – China, Japan and the Soviet Union – of whom the last can claim to be a Eurasian great power. Meanwhile one by one the fall of Singapore, of Dien Bien Phu and the Vietnam war have marked the decline and eventual exit of Britain, France and the United States as major powers in continental Asia even though the United States remains a superpower at large in the Pacific area.

Conclusion

It was almost inevitable that the 15 year growth in trade between the industrialised countries would eventually surmount the ideological differences between the Communist and non-Communist industrialised states. The closer commercial contact between the two halves of Europe can only be understood within this wider non-ideological context. At a time when the Unitied States is reviewing the nature of her European commitment nobody should overlook that the Soviet Union has never been more committed to Europe than at this moment. In the past this commitment was to secure the inviolability of her western frontiers. The Warsaw Pact was therefore concerned with maintaining a form of Soviet military hegemony over Eastern Europe. Today the Soviet Union has staked the future economic prosperity of her people on the steady integration of her economy with that of the rest of Europe.

At the same time the Soviet Union perceives herself as a Eurasian as well as European power. She has therefore over recent years forged considerable commercial links with India, Bangladesh, the United Arab Republic, Syria, Iraq, Algeria and Morocco. She also plans to expand her ties with Afghanistan, Iran, Turkey and Pakistan. In other words a definite Soviet sphere of influence is being staked out in the Middle East and South Asian area. The Soviet Union's ambition to extend her influence in the Middle East is of course a legacy which she inherited from Tzarist Russia and as in the past brings her into conflict with the grand design of other Eruopean states, notably France, not to mention the United States. But her wish to extend her commercial and diplomatic influence in southern Asia is something relatively new. Ever since the British withdrew from the Indian sub-continent there has been something of a power vacuum in the area. The successful Soviet diplomatic intervention at Tashkent symbolised the beginning of Soviet commercial and diplomatic ascendancy in the area. Today the Soviet Union has begun to fulfil her ambition to become not simply a European but a Eurasian power, something quite distinct from her status as one of the world's two superpowers. With a massive nuclear arsenal and a million men under arms on both her western and eastern frontiers respectively when her East European satellite armies are included in the calculations, her superpower capacity is not seriously in question.

5 The United States, Europe and Latin America

The U.S. and Europe

Ten years ago the idea of encouraging the creation of a strong and prosperous West European community seemed a very reasonable proposition to most Americans. Not only would such a community be able to treat with the United States on a more equal footing but, it was always assumed, it would also shoulder some of the responsibilities of maintaining the free world system. It was even conceivable that Britain would so influence the Community that the special relationship could be extended to the new Western Europe community. Unfortunately General de Gaulle did not want any special relationship, certainly not with the United States, and saw quite clearly that if he kept Britain out for the next decade such a relationship would probably never develop. Subsequent events seem to confirm his view.

Ten years ago Britain's gross national product was about 25 per cent greater than that of France; today it is 25 per cent less than that of France which has, broadly speaking, drawn up the rules of the club to maintain that sort of advantage more or less permanently. Moreover, France remains as jealous of American power and influence as at any time in the past, as can be seen in her virulently anti-American monetary policies. By and large she is skilful enough to disguise her own interests under the cloak of West European unity of which the best example is the Common Agricultural Policy, conceived as a means towards greater cohesion but in practice a gigantic international relief programme for French farmers. But France aside, apart from the general attitude of chauvinism abroad, there are some very particular differences which plague the relationship between the United States and the European Community as of now. Some of these differences – like the Common Agricultural Policy and the EEC preferences with Mediterranean countries – have become well known from regular airing, others remain obscure.

The underlying theme which runs through U.S. dissatisfaction with the European Community, and equally with Japan, is that the United States has succoured them both long enough. After twenty-eight years of 'reconstruction' not only are they both prosperous, self-confident and secure but they believe themselves to have, to use Roy Jenkins' phrase, 'come of age'. In American eyes, Western Europe must begin to realise that it is time for her to assume her global responsibilities, notably in the fields of defence, trade and monetary affairs. So far, the American version runs, the European Community seems to have become content to pursue its commercial interests heedless of the trend toward exclusive and competing world blocs.

U.S. Grievances

(1) *Agricultural preferences.* By far the most serious source of friction between the United States and Western Europe stems from the EEC's protectionist Common Agricultural Policy and its special preferential trading agreements with non-members. While both these measures clearly violate Article 24 of the General Agreement on Trade and Tariffs (GATT), a majority of GATT members are already dependent on the enlarged Community which effectively prevents them from lining up against the Community unless their own vital interest dictate them to do so. The need to seriously modify the CAP has long been recognised, and the EEC's Commissioner for External Relations, Sir Christopher Soames, has now stated bluntly that if the coming GATT negotiations are to suceed the CAP must be amended to meet American objections at least halfway. The trouble is that without the CAP and the Common External Tariff the Community can hardly be said to exist – certainly this has

been the French and, to a lesser extent, the German position for some years. Moreover, both policies were seen as the only available means of pursuing integration at that time, and have by their very nature promoted European self-sufficiency, in agriculture especially, at the expense of third parts like the United States, Canada, Australia and New Zealand.

(2) *Industrial discrimination.* Largely thanks to the Kennedy Round, industrial tariffs between the world's developed countries are not especially high. However, the United States is not only concerned about tariffs but also European subsidies to industry and the possibility of Regional Policies growing into something along the lines of a Common Industrial Policy comparable in scale and influence to the Common Agricultural Policy.

(3) *Monetary policy conflict.* The United States' position is baldly that monetary reform is inseparable from moves towards trade liberalisation. For the moment it specifically favours a system of par values which are easily adjustable. The European Community is inclined to interpret the United States' position as a means of exporting U.S. inflation. Since the Community also tends to treat monetary policy as a separate issue there has been understandably painfully slow progress on the subject of monetary reform within the Committee of Twenty industrial powers.

(4) *Defence responsibility.* The big question, as ever, is, who shall bear the costs? While Professor Eugene Rostow wisely counsels that military forces should be deployed only for security reasons and kept out of balance of payments considerations, the fact that the United States provides 90 per cent of the West's nuclear capacity, stations 300,000 men in Europe and spends $7 billion on overseas military expenditure and foreign aid is bound to make the U.S. electorate want to improve the cost sharing arrangements. Though the 'no wheat, no troops' lobby gains increasing ground in the United States only the West Germans seem jittery about the prospects of major U.S. troop withdrawals.

(5) *Barriers to Japan.* The United States is by far the largest export market for Japan with whom it has a major trade deficit, in 1972 it accounted for two-thirds of the U.S.'s total overseas trade deficit in fact. If Western Europe

were less discriminating over Japanese exports, the United States argues, this deficit would rapidly and substantially decline.

(6) *Resistance to U.S. investment.* The European Community, and especially France, wants checks on the extent of U.S. investment in Europe and much greater control of those companies which already operate extensively in Europe. Indeed, the EEC will push for a code to govern the behaviour of multinationals within the framework of GATT.

European Grievances

Although European grievances against the United States are less substantial in content than those of the United States against Europe they are almost as numerous.

(1) *Agricultural import quotas.* Like Europe the United States has practised considerable protectionism in agriculture. Section 22 of the American Adjustment Act allows for the introduction of quotas in commodities such as cheese or beef which very effectively limits foreign competition at will. The noticeable aspect of these quotas, however, is that they have very little serious effect on European exports.

(2) *Industrial tariffs.* According to the GATT figures chosen by Sir Christopher Soames, the average industrial tariff of the original European Community stood at 6 per cent compared with the United States' 7 per cent and Japan's nearly 10 per cent. The Europeans complain that some U.S. industrial tariffs remain at over 25 per cent. This is true and can be remedied but the averages show that the United States also has a far greater proportion of low tariffs than the European Community. However, if duty-free goods are included and the average industrial tariffs are weighted according to world trade as a whole, the United States has a slightly lower figure, 6.02 per cent, than the Six's, 6.07 per cent. At this moment, the truth is that as long as major currencies float as freely as they do now tariffs are obviously much less important.

(3) *Non-tariff barriers.* The target of much European criticism is the Buy America Act which in practice is applied almost entirely in the field of defence equipment. It accounts

for less than 1 per cent of all U.S. foreign trade. It should be noted that European countries frequently follow similar practices. The chief difference is that they do not pass statutes about it. Thus the British Government habitually grants contracts to British computer companies whatever the foreign tenders, as Honeywell have found to their cost recently. Nevertheless there is some truth in the charge that the U.S. Government has strengthened arrangements to give American products a privileged position in government procurement. The present U.S. Trade Reform Bill grants the President power to revoke the Buy America Act.

(4) *Self-limitation measures.* The most notable example are those 'imposed' by the U.S. Government on Community steel imports.

(5) *Anti-dumping duties.* According to the Europeans, the United States has applied these duties increasingly and more frequently than any other industrialised country. The answer to this is that the United States is one of the few countries capable of retaliating effectively when dumping takes place. New Zealand, for instance, can do very little when the European Community dumps its surplus butter on a potential commercial market like the Soviet Union.

(6) *Monetary policy.* The European Community, at least in theory, favours strict controls and a fixed parity and resents what it regards as the U.S. export of inflation through huge deficits abroad. Moreover, it argues that the United States should remedy her deficit with Japan without taking any action detrimental to Europe on the presumed assumption that nations should balance their trade with each country separately. Such views have no foundation in economics however desirable they may sometimes be politically.

Atlantic Gaullism

If President Nixon's trade bill and monetary reform proposals are to lead down the road to multilateral co-operation all these issues must be faced and overcome. No issue can afford to be sacrosanct. Above all, it will take time. However regretfully, one cannot escape the conclusion that the only counter to European Gaullism is a Nixon-Kissinger brand of

American Gaullism. By his separate accommodations with China and the Soviet Union the President has shown he has the temper for pursuing a unilateral path. Whether or not the present ominous trends continue will depend in large part on Europe's reactions to U.S. proposals in the GATT negotiations. Meanwhile, if friction between the United States and the European Community grows, the Western alliance will become more and more unstable. As long as the EEC remained a moderate-sized grouping its irresponsibility could be overlooked. Now that the EEC is enlarged a constant dialogue must be maintained between it and the United States if the Western alliance is to survive in any meaningful form.

The U.S. and Latin America

With the notable exception of Cuba, almost every major Latin American government was in 1974 conservatively orientated, while those of Brazil, the Argentine, Chile and Uruguay were governed either directly or indirectly by generals. The truth is that Latin America's social problems are so acute that any attempt to grapple with them wholeheartedly invites intervention by conservative forces. For in spite of an increased growth rate (2.3 per cent in the 1950s compared with 4.5 per cent in the 1960s) most Latin Americans remain desperately poor. Not only is the average income per head around $600 (the U.S. average is six times greater) but the richest 5 per cent account for 40 per cent of the national income, while the poorest 40 per cent receive only 10 per cent of the national cake. Such terrifying inequalities are matched by a corresponding vulnerability to outside, especially U.S., domination. For although Latin America constitutes a continent with a diverse series of external relations, there is but one overriding relationship, that with the United States.

Long before the Declaration of Buenos Aires (July 1970) called for closer relations between Latin America and the European Community, conflict within the inter-American system had led to a conscious attempt by many Latin American countries to seek a counterweight to U.S. influence. By the early 1960s nearly all the major Latin

American countries had established diplomatic missions in Brussels. In 1968, the Italian Government, which with substantial trade and investment with Latin America in general and Argentina in particular had become the champion of Latin American interests within the Community, submitted a memorandum to the Commission on EEC—Latin American relations. The memorandum included strong criticism of the EEC Common Agricultural Policy, particularly the harmful affects of the CAP on the Argentine economy. In response to this initiative the Commission prepared a report for the Council of Ministers on EEC—Latin American relations. It became clear from the report that, at least in the mind of Ralf Dahrendorf, the Commissioner then responsible for External Relations, that the EEC and Latin America might form a useful alliance in moderating U.S. economic domination of the Western hemisphere. The degree of that domination is still not fully appreciated outside Latin America.

The foundations of U.S. economic hegemony in Latin America are twofold. First, the United States is the source of 70 per cent of all foreign investment; secondly, the United States remains by far the largest market (30 per cent) for Latin American exports as well as being the major source (35 per cent) of Latin American imports. These percentages, although they amply illustrate the overwhelming U.S. presence, cannot convey the degree to which this presence determines the economic climate of most Latin American countries. Why, for instance, does Latin America buy such a high proportion of its imports from the United States which is by and large the most expensive supplier? The underlying answer is because the United States is the most important creditor in Latin America. Although the United States recently had a trade deficit with Latin America running around $150 million, the annual net outflow of foreign exchange from Latin America to the United States has been about $275 million. This arises from the fact, first, that U.S. companies provide 75 per cent of direct investment, and secondly, that private investment is matched by official U.S. aid which is generally tied to U.S. suppliers (between 1960—1968 both U.S. aid and U.S. private investment to

Latin America each amounted to $6,000 million). Some economists have estimated the increased cost to Latin America of tying U.S. aid at about 24 per cent, though such a figure is arguable. What is not arguable is that service charges actually cancel out a large proportion of the original capital contribution, which in the meantime has conferred a competitive advantage on the foreign investor, that of indebtedness by the recipient.

In these circumstances, so entirely favourable to the United States, it is hardly surprising that 50 per cent of all capital accumulation arising from the direct investment of advanced countries in developing countries derives from Latin America (which also accounts for 60 per cent of all foreign investment in manufacturing, generally more profitable for the outside investor though agricultural investment is what most Latin American societies need). Because of the favourable economic climate U.S. petroleum investment in Latin America is still higher than in the Middle East. Thus the cumulative effects of U.S. official agencies and U.S. companies in the region has until recently constituted a preferential trade area for the United States in the Western hemisphere. There are, however, signs of a gradual decline in U.S. dominance relative to the EEC and Japan, for instance, though nothing remotely approaching a challenge to U.S. predominance in the area.

First, in the 1960s Latin American imports from the United States have fallen from 45 per cent in 1960 to 36 per cent in 1970. Secondly, between 1960–1969 Latin American exports to the developed countries increased by 45 per cent, while those to the United States went up by 10 per cent and to EFTA (including Britain) by 20 per cent. By contrast exports to the Six went up by 72 per cent and to Japan by 350 per cent. Putting these percentages into perspective by taking account of the base level from which they grew we find that in the 1960s the EEC share of Latin American exports rose from 18 per cent to 21 per cent while Japan's increased from 3 per cent to 6 per cent. In the early 1970s both Japan and the EEC (chiefly Germany and France) have contrived to gain some ground at U.S. expense. Already the EEC is comfortably the second largest market for Latin

American exports, and growing at a faster rate than the U.S. market. The growth of EEC—Latin American trade has been especially noticeable with the countries which comprise the southern cone of the continent, namely Argentina and Chile. Yet all is not well with EEC—Latin American relations, especially if the enlarged Community hopes to provide some form of counterbalancing influence to U.S. dominance.

There are two principal areas of conflict between Latin America and the EEC both of which are concerned with tropical or temperate zone agricultural goods. They involve, first, the question of tariffs, principally the CAP, and secondly, the preferential arrangements which the EEC has made with neighbouring Mediterranean and African associated states. The enlargement of the EEC, and especially British entry, has not helped. Not only is the British market likely to become more restricted to Latin American agricultural exports but the possible addition of various new Commonwealth associates from Africa and possibly the Caribbean with preferential arrangements will tend to penalise many Latin American agricultural exports.

The resolution of Buenos Aires of 1970 included a clause which supported bilateral negotiations between the EEC and Latin American countries. By and large, with the notable exception of the Andean Group (comprising Bolivia, Chile, Colombia, Ecuador, Peru and Venezuela), this has characterised the Latin American approach. Thus Argentina negotiated a treaty with the EEC in 1970 to mitigate the effects of the CAP on her beef exports as well as reducing tariffs on thirteen other products. By June 1971 permanent machinery was established for an annual dialogue between the EEC Commission and Latin American ambassadors in Brussels. But adequate machinery for consultation is one thing, policy accord quite another. In the wake of EEC enlargement with its steady extension of European self-sufficiency in agriculture, there is the risk of Latin American hopes of lessening their dependence on the United States, by fostering closer links with the EEC, becoming fatally dashed. Should the EEC fail to find a way to accommodate Latin American interests either in the approaching GATT negotiations or by generous direct concessions then the rift between the rich and the poor

will have become significantly wider. For one of the lessons
which post-war economic history has seemed to suggest is
that only a diversified set of economic relationships with the
advanced countries will save a less advanced country from
perpetuating its subordinate position. The moral seems to be
that nations, like people, should avoid relying too heavily on
a single partner. The least Europe owes Latin America – and
Africa and Asia for that matter – is to make such a choice
possible.

The EEC, the U.S. and the Caribbean

As long ago as July 1972 it was decided by CARIFTA (the
Caribbean Free Trade Association) that it would negotiate as
a group with the EEC, seeking special arrangements to
safeguard the vital interests of particular islands where
necessary. Like the thirteen African Commonwealth
countries eligible for association, Barbados, Guyana, Jamaica,
Trinidad and Tobago must choose between either the
Yaoundé or Arusha types of association, or negotiate special
bilateral arrangements. The eight British Caribbean dependencies have already accepted association under Clause 4 of
the Treaty of Rome, granting them preferential access to the
EEC and the European Development Fund (EDF) aid. In
order to help the four determine what should be their
negotiating posture with the EEC, CARIFTA sent an official
mission to tour East and West Africa as well as the member
countries of the current Yaoundé Association. Since then
there have been numerous meetings held in both Brussels and
elsewhere. Underlying these diplomatic junkets is the stark
reality that the effects of EEC enlargement on the Commonwealth Caribbean have been sketchily calculated and only
dimly understood.

The first overall assessment of the possible consequences
for the Commonwealth Caribbean were made in 1967 by the
West India Committee, which published a report assessing the
possible consequences for the various export commodities.
Apart from the Lancaster House agreement on sugar (which
in Protocol 22 attached to the Accession Treaty commits the
enlarged EEC to negotiate substitute arrangements for the
sugar producers of the developing Commonwealth when the

Commonwealth Sugar Agreement expires at the end of 1974) there is little to indicate what the enlarged EEC is likely to offer and what the prospective Caribbean 'associables' intend. Before examining the individual circumstances of the four independent Caribbean islands it might be useful to make some general points covering specific commodities and the overall pattern of CARIFTA trade.

As is well known, the economies of most of the Caribbean islands developed on a bilateral basis with the colonial power. In spite of the remarkable recent growth in intra-CARIFTA trade (including moves towards the creation of a Caribbean Common Market with a common external tariff) and the increase in exports from the main islands to North America (especially in manufactured goods), Britain remains the major market for the Caribbean's most important agricultural exports. This fact alone explains why the Caribbean four must examine closely the possibilities of association in spite of their generally low level of current trade with the EEC.

For not only must Britain adapt to the EEC's generally protectionist policies on commodities such as sugar and bananas but the Caribbean islands are peculiarly dependent on a handful of agricultural commodities. Furthermore, not only is agriculture the chief provider of employment (500,000 work in the sugar industry alone), but it is also the largest source of foreign exchange. Even among the smaller islands, which will at least be offered preferential access, there will be a need for firm quotas if considerable social dislocation is to be prevented, notably in the Windward and Leeward Islands heavily reliant on bananas, and St Kitts equally dependent on sugar and facing the prospect of greatly expanded French sugar beet acreage.

In weighing up the pros and cons for the Caribbean four, the trade access and aid advantages of the Yaoundé type association must be set against the absence of protection for their sugar, rum and banana exports. Moreover, the CAP specifically discriminates against key Caribbean products such as sugar, molasses, citrus, rice and tobacco, of which only the first two are covered by Protocol 22, and then only until the end of 1974. In the case of bananas (not covered by the CAP), Germany, France and Italy have traditionally made special bulk purchases, usually with Central American states which are likely to undercut Jamaican and Windward Islands' bananas with or without association. Similarly, although rum would enter duty free under a Yaoundé association agreement it would face indirect taxes on the French market, plus competition from the French Caribbean rum producers.

But the really major reservation shared by each of the Caribbean four in greater or lesser degree is that by joining a vast Euro-African trade bloc they may find themselves discriminated against by the United States – even now the most important market for Guyana, Jamaica and Trinidad and Tobago. Already the U.S. has threatened to withold its GSP (General Preference Scheme) from any country which offers reverse preferences, as do the EEC association agreements. Ideally, the Caribbean four would like expanded access into both EEC and North American markets, especially for their alumina and petroleum products, but it is not yet clear which of the general preference schemes, that of the EEC or the projected American one would benefit them most – even whether the EEC will adapt Britain's preference scheme, markedly more generous in agricultural exports than that of the EEC.

In the light of the general trend in trade, aid and investment, which suggests increasing links between North America and the Caribbean islands as well as among the Caribbean islands themselves, the four independent Caribbean islands are probably best advised to negotiate separate trade agreements rather than opt for a form of association.

At the moment Jamaica is the only one of the four which seems favourably disposed towards becoming a full associate. However, until some firm long-term arrangements on sugar has been reached none of the four is likely to make any irrevocable decision. Meanwhile the particular circumstances of the four, including their external trade patterns, deserve close examination.

Barbados

The value of sugar to Barbados is around ten times that of any other export commodity and represents 70 per cent of its annual exports (tourism currently represents by far the most important source of foreign exchange but suffers from considerable fluctuations in demand). While Britain accounts for 30 per cent of Barbadian imports, the United States 20 per cent and Canada 10 per cent, around 40 per cent of Barbadian exports go to Britain, 30 per cent to the Commonwealth (excluding Britain and Canada) and 20 per cent to the United States. Significantly, between 1968 and 1970 Barbados exports to Britain declined from 60 per cent to 40 per cent while her exports to other parts of the Commonwealth (apart from Britain and Canada) increased from 10 per cent to 30 per cent.

Guyana

Like Barbados, sugar is of the utmost importance to Guyana, followed by bauxite and alumina. Unlike Barbados, the United States has displaced Britain as Guyana's chief export market (as it has also become for Jamaica and Trinidad and Tobago). Indeed, more than 60 per cent of all Guyana's exports currently go to destinations in the Western hemisphere, Canada's imports alone equalling those of Britain. Nevertheless, Britain remains Guyana's major market for sugar, worth almost double that of her sugar exports to the United States (which only began a decade or so ago when U.S.–Cuban relations were severed). Britain has a major financial stake in Guyana's sugar producing industry.

Jamaica

The largest and most populous member of CARIFTA, Jamaica, like Barbados and Guyana, is heavily dependent on sugar, which accounts for 23 per cent of its total annual exports. Out of a total production of around 360,000 tons, 300,000 tons are exported, of which 230,000 tons goes to Britain and a mere 60,000 to the United States. Second to sugar in importance to Jamaica comes bananas, of which almost the entire crop is shipped to Britain and which is seriously at risk with the creation of an enlarged EEC. Should Jamaica apply for association under the Yaoundé agreement she will require special arrangements guaranteeing her minimum export quantities for both sugar and bananas. Meanwhile Jamaica's trade is steadily switching away from Britain.

Already her exports to the United States are double those to
Britain, followed by Canada, EFTA and CARIFTA (in the
first half of 1972 Jamaica's exports to CARIFTA grew by 75
per cent). With 60 per cent of her trade being carried out
with the dollar area and exports to North America running at
twice the level of her exports to the sterling area (exports to
the EEC are negligible), Jamaica would have to think twice
before becoming an associate member of the EEC.

Trinidad and Tobago

Thanks to its petroleum industry which provides 75 per cent
of its export income, Trinidad and Tobago is the only
member of CARIFTA which is not dependent on agricultural
exports. Trinidad and Tobago's three next most important
exports, sugar, asphalt and cocoa, between them account
for less than 10 per cent of her export earnings. Dwarfing all
other export markets is the United States, which buys more
than 50 per cent of all Trinidad and Tobago's exports. Britain
comes next with 10 per cent. Although Trinidad and Tobago
might wish to modify her almost total dependence on the
North American petroleum market there is little likelihood of
her taking the risk of doing anything which would harm her
relations with the United States.

In the light, therefore, of their increasingly preponderant
trade and investment links with the United States, and the
uncertainty of the advantages accruing under the EEC terms
of association, there must be every likelihood of Barbados,
Guyana, Jamaica, and Trinidad and Tobago turning down
association with the EEC. They may nevertheless seek
special bilateral arrangements in an attempt to ease the
transition of various key commodities such as sugar and
bananas.

Conclusion

The overall trade and investment trends in the Western
hemisphere suggest that although a continuing underlying need
for radical economic and social reform is likely to persist
throughout the whole of Latin America, almost entirely

unsatisfied, U.S. dominance will continue in political as well as economic terms. In the Caribbean, U.S. influence is likely to grow in spite of Fidel Castro's appeal to the deprived sections of the population. The influence of both the EEC and Japan looks like remaining marginal in Latin America for some time to come.

6 The Re-emergence of Japan as an East Asian and World Power

As the third richest economic power and the fourth most active trading power in the world, it was not unexpected that when Dr Kissinger announced President Nixon's desire to frame a new Atlantic Charter it should include Japan. Not only has the mutual interdependence of the three major industrial powers in the non-Communist world — the United States, Japan and Western Europe — become more apparent but the necessity to create a more complementary and less potentially fractious economic order has become urgent. This is the more so against the background of the increasing political 'multipolarity' in international relations where there are several centres of world power. Japan's own emerging economic role can only be properly understood by tracing the history of her economic relations with the United States.

U.S. — Japanese Trade

At the beginning of the American occupation Japan's foreign trade was overwhelmingly tied to the United States. In 1946, for instance, Japan's trade with the United States accounted for 65 per cent of her exports and 86 per cent of her imports. Today these figures have shrunk to 30 per cent and 25 per cent respectively. During the intervening period, with protection against external competition and a centrally directed capitalist system, Japan has grown to her present position among the world's major industrial nations. The imbalance in favour of Japan in recent years has, under American pressure, led to revaluation of the yen (currently floating) and a series of export controls designed to reduce Japan's trade surplus by around $1000million (about £400 m.) annually. However, if President Nixon gains approval for his proposed 'safeguard clause' in his trade bill, which would allow him to raise U.S. tariffs against Japanese imports if he deems it necessary, there has been a strong suggestion that Japan would end her decontrol of imports and inward capital investment. Japan equally adamantly opposes a similar 'safeguard clause' in the planned EEC–Japan trade treaty.

An Advanced Economy

Japan's economic relations with both the United States and Western Europe are crucial not only to herself but to the whole future pattern of trade between industrialised countries. The extent to which Japan is integrated into the network of the industrialised world is seen in the fact that — after the United States — Australia and Canada are Japan's principal trading partners. With only about 12 per cent of her trade conducted with the enlarged European Community, there is considerable potential for growth in Japan's trade with Europe. Certainly the American view is that if the EEC admitted more Japanese manufactures it would take the heat out of the American dispute with Japan.

As with the other major industrialised nations, the vast majority of Japanese exports, 94 per cent in fact, comprises manufactured goods, which also account for around 30 per cent of Japanese imports. Japan's other principal import categories are raw materials, 36 per cent, and foodstuffs, 14 per cent. Before the war textiles accounted for half of all Japanese exports. Today they only account for around 14 per cent. Instead of textiles it is heavy machinery and engineering equipment which account for nearly half of all Japanese exports. Among these, ships and electrical machines figure prominently. In the degree to which her trade is concentrated on the exchange of manufactured goods with other industrialised countries, Japan's economy is typical of an advanced industrial nation.

Asian–Japanese Trade

In the period before the war, when Japan was pursuing the policy of so-called co-prosperity in Asia, Japan's major markets were all in Asia. Thus in 1934–36, for example, Japan's trade with Asia (including Korea and Formosa, then under Japanese control) accounted for 64 per cent of her exports and 53 per cent of her imports. China alone accounted for 17 per cent of Japan's exports. Today, in spite of a considerable increase in Japanese trade in South-East Asia, notably with Malaysia, Singapore and Indonesia, Asian countries account for no more than a third of Japan's total foreign trade. Japan's trade with her giant neighbour China was only about 2 per cent of her total foreign trade in 1969, reflecting a thus far unconsummated relationship between the two countries. However, in 1972 it grew dramatically and is expected to continue its rapid expansion. The situation is complicated by the fact that Japan is anxious to develop good relations with both the Soviet Union *and* China, two countries who are in open dispute. In spite of the fact that no peace treaty has ever been signed between the Soviet Union and Japan (largely because of the Soviet Union's refusal to return four of the northernmost Japanese islands) there has been a steady growth in trade which was worth about £400 million in 1972 (cf. around £300 m. with China).

If Japan's links with Asia seem insubstantial at the moment compared with pre-war days there are signs she is recommencing her historic role as an influential East Asian power. Ever since the Japanese Prime Minister, Tanaka Kakuois, made the diplomatic break with Chiang Kai-shek, Sino-Japanese relations have been placed on a completely new footing. The assumption in Tokyo seems to be that Taiwan will eventually return to the bosom of mainland China's political control but that Japan will be able to maintain close economic links (she already has a substantial stake as well as a preferred export position) providing her with a promising ecomomic beachhead with China. In the wake of American military commitments to both Korea and Indo-China, Japan has been unobtrusively expanding not only her trade but also her investment stake. With her highly advanced technology this often takes the form of technical and licensing links, which, together with her direct and indirect investment, has given Japan a far greater influence in the area than is immediately apparent. If Japan's trade with Australia and New Zealand is included, her trade with Asia already exceeds her total trade with North America. The underlying truth seems to be that Japan's re-emergence as an East Asian power, made possible because of her acceptance of American nuclear protection, extends beyond Asia to the entire Pacific basin.

A Pacific Power

Behind the mood for promoting closer political and economic co-operation between the Asian-Pacific nations lies the stark fact that Japan conducts 80 per cent of her foreign trade with countries which border the Pacific. Moreover, Japan needs raw materials every bit as much as the less developed countries need her technology and investment. For the present Japan is drawing heavily from the great natural resources of Australia and Canada but she has already turned her attention to new areas. Although it has just begun, Japanese businessmen are now making dramatic inroads into Latin America, an area which has been a traditional preserve of American business. In Brazil, which boasts a community of more than 500,000 people of Japanese extraction, Japan is busily investing in shipbuilding, steel, automobiles, textiles, electronics and farm equipment. Unconfirmed reports claim that Mitsubishi plans to invest £1,000 m. In Peru, the Japan Petroleum Development Corporation is financing a £100m.-plus pipeline vaulting the Andes and linking the Amazon basin with the Pacific coast; in Venezuela, Japan has agreed to finance the construction of a £40 m. aluminium plant at Guyana; in Argentina, Japan hopes to electrify the state-owned railways.

Matching her commercial expansion, Japan has been extending her programme of economic aid until she is now the fourth largest world aid donor, most of it untied. Her most notable success in this field has been the Asian Development Bank which she conceived and substantially funds. Deeply sensitive to local national sentiment, Japan has so far proved to be an exemplarily responsible power in the Pacific region. Whether she will prove as imaginative, magnanimous and constructive in her relations with her industrialised peers remains an important unanswered question.

At the end of the 1960s 52 per cent of Japan's exports went to developed countries, compared with 43 per cent to developing countries, and 5 per cent to Communist countries.

Hopefully, by the end of the 1970s, both the developing countries and the Communist countries will have increased their participation in Japan's prosperity. In the 1960s Japan's exports increased at about twice the rate of world exports; in the 1970s it is just possible that she may have to settle for a slower export performance as her contribution to world stability. At the very least a higher degree of reciprocity will be expected from her by her major trading partners.

The Pacific Commonwealth

Within the next year or so more than two-thirds of the Commonwealth's membership are likely to join the EEC as associate members, linked by far more demanding ties than the Commonwealth system has ever contemplated. It has been remarked by more than one critic of the Commonwealth that as far as British interests and trade figures are concerned, it is the old white Commonwealth which constitutes the central core of the Commonwealth system. Such criticism overlooks the importance that Commonwealth trade has played in the development of Asian and African members. Nevertheless, it is true that two-thirds of all intra-Commonwealth trade is carried out with Britain and 50 per cent of Britain's imports from the Commonwealth come from Canada, Australia and New Zealand, which in turn absorb 50 per cent of all British exports to the Commonwealth.

Canada*

In Ottawa's eyes the enlarged EEC is important not only as the world's largest trading unit but also as a significant alternative source of investment capital at a time when Canada is uncomfortably dependent on U.S. investment. Following a post-war boom, when Canadian goods were required to help rebuild a war-ravaged Europe, Canada is now suffering increasing handicaps in trade with Western Europe. Not only have there been restrictions on the import of Canadian aluminium and newsprint, but the EEC's Common Agricul-

*The Middle East war aftermath, by raising the price of oil, has made much of Canada's oil reserves extractable on a commercial basis; by so doing it has greatly enhanced Canada's future overall economic prospects.

tural Policy has both restricted Canadian agricultural exports to Europe and caused the dumping of subsidised wheat and other cereals on Canada's alternate markets. Moreover, the proliferation of EEC preferential arrangements with Mediterranean and African countries has undermined Canadian exports in these regions.

The effects of EEC enlargement on Canada stem from two main sources: the Common External Tariff (CET) and the Common Agricultural Policy (CAP). Britain is, at present, Canada's second largest export market, accounting for $1.5 billion in 1972. This was approximately equal to Canada's exports to the Six, but a long way behind the $11 billion-worth of goods exported to the United States. Following Britain's entry, only about 36 per cent of Canadian exports to the enlarged EEC enter duty free, compared with 94 per cent previously. Today 64 per cent of all Canadian goods going to the Nine must face tariffs, loss of Commonwealth preferences and suffer reverse preferences in favour of EEC members.

However, it is the indirect rather than the direct consequences of EEC enlargement which most concern Canada. Even excluding intra-Community trade the enlarged EEC accounts for 25 per cent of world trade compared with about 20 per cent for the United States. Furthermore, nearly fifty of the ninety-one members of the General Agreement on Trade and Tariffs are likely to be members or associate members of the EEC. Clearly, the attitude of the enlarged EEC towards liberalising the world trading system could be crucial for future world prosperity. Should the EEC perpetuate its more protectionist policies, in due course it will almost certainly induce retaliatory protectionist legislation from the United States, which could be a severe blow for Canada, which sells 75 per cent of its exports to the United States providing it with a £1,000 m. surplus in 1972. (70 per cent of Canada's total trade is with the U.S.) Moreover, the United States controls a substantial share of the Canadian economy including 45 per cent of Canadian manufacturing, 56 per cent of mining and smelting and 60 per cent of the petroleum and natural gas industries. Canada is thus among the most vulnerable to any slide into protectionism.

Australia

In the case of Australia, only around 8 per cent of exports are put at risk as a result of British entry into the EEC and the effects are concentrated in three main industries – dairying, fruit farming and sugar production. Britain still accounts for some 60 per cent of Australian butter exports and 20 per cent of its cheese exports. Altogether, Britain buys 35 per cent of Australia's entire milk production, which makes the CAP's restriction of Australia to a merely residual supplier a very serious matter. The special arrangements gained by New Zealand, especially for butter, and the entry of Denmark (a major dairy exporter) hardly help Australian producers.

Australian fruit, whether it be fresh, canned or dried, will face a variety of tariffs and restraints, and areas requiring large-scale investment for irrigation or other purposes will be particularly hard hit. Britain at present absorbs around 50 per cent of Australian fruit exports. Sugar exports to Britain have already shrunk from 54 per cent in 1961–62 to 27 per cent in 1970–71, and the prospects of continuing sugar exports after the termination of the Commonwealth Sugar Agreement in 1974 are almost non-existent.

Apart from these three industries, the Australian economy is not likely to be greatly affected. Since the early 1960s, when 75 per cent of Australia's exports were farm products, the mineral trade has increased tenfold and manufactured exports have quadrupled in value. The mineral boom has enabled Australia to diversify both her economy and overseas markets in a manner not open to New Zealand. By 1970, Australia's major export markets, in order of importance, were: Japan, United States, Britain and New Zealand. Japan takes Australian exports worth twice as much as those to the United States. Australian industrialists and businessmen have one serious worry however – whether British capital inflow will be checked and, if so, will it be replaced by French, German, Japanese or American capital?

New Zealand

The efforts of the British Government to protect New Zealand from the possibly disastrous effects of British entry are well known. New Zealand's basic requirement in seeking to protect its dairy exports has been a continuing arrangement subject to review. The quantities stated in the arrangement are intended to cover the first five years. Until January 1978, New Zealand has an assured outlet for its butter and cheese, although the quantities with guaranteed access will be progressively reduced. By 1977, the quantity of butter will have been reduced to 80 per cent of the 1973 figure, and in the case of cheese it will be reduced to 20 per cent, with no guarantees thereafter.

One of the most important assurances that the EEC has given New Zealand is to discontinue dumping surplus dairy products, which has hitherto prevented New Zealand from effectively developing many new markets. In spite of intensive exports, and the switch from dairying to beef, Britain remains New Zealand's largest export market with no immediate substitute in sight. As late as 1972 the Nine absorbed 43 per cent of New Zealand's exports, with New Zealand buying 38 per cent of its imports from the Nine in return.* Though each of the three Pacific Commonwealth dominions (one of them is in fact a Commonwealth) are anxious to carve independent foreign policies, they are almost inevitably gravitating closer towards the United States and Japan. France's determination to test her atomic weapons in the Pacific and Britain's half-hearted protest, have undoubtedly strengthened fellow feeling among the Pacific countries at the expense of their bonds with Europe.

---

*The spectacular increase in oil prices following in the wake of the Middle East war (1973) may trigger off an oil and coal energy boom for New Zealand by making her Antarctic fields economic for the first time.

7 The Outlines of a Chinese Economic Foreign Policy

With some justification it has been claimed that when it comes down to whom she does business with China is as pragmatic as any capitalist state. But though this may be broadly true it cannot disguise the profound influence of Maoism on the extent, nature and direction of Chinese foreign trade and its close connection with the overall objectives of Chinese foreign policy.

The Domestic Roots of Foreign Policy

To begin with, of all the world's major economic powers China remains the most self-sufficient. Even today after some well publicised diplomatic rapproachements with both the United States and Japan her foreign trade accounts for less than 3 per cent of her gross national product. Such a degree of self-reliance arose partly from China's determination to give priority to labour intensive agriculture rather than some form of highly capitalised industrialisation with its attendant appetite for vast energy and raw material resources. But there was a further reason which lay outside China's ability to control or decide. That reason was the almost total isolation of China from the West by trade and diplomatic embargo for twenty years. For half that time she was also isolated from any form of assistance from the Soviet Union, whom she had previously relied upon heavily. Not surprisingly she has evolved a uniquely decentralised and self-reliant domestic economy.

Now that diplomacy has paved the way, China is free to pursue a more expansionist trade policy, but on her own terms, which means a very closely balanced export—import pattern with each country. Moreover, as a result of her harsh experience, China will never again readily rely on a single economic partner as she once relied so utterly on the Soviet Union. This theme has deeply affected China's whole approach to her external economic relations which are characterised by a deliberate diversity sometimes mistaken for mere pragmatism. Hence also her deep-seated suspicion of what she terms 'the hegemonists', the United States and the Soviet Union. The manner in which China has consistently supported any nation or bloc which stood up to either one of the superpowers has been a striking feature of her foreign policy for some time. As the original champion of polycentrism within the international Communist movement, this should surprise nobody.

The Premisses of Chinese Foreign Policy

China has always instinctively felt itself to be the premier Asian nation. This feeling arose not only because of China's great size and vast population but also from an appreciation of the heritage of an ancient and still flourishing culture. Building on these instincts of her people, China's Communist leaders for nearly a quarter of a century devoted themselves to creating a distinctive Maoist society free from any sort of outside hegemony. However, as in the 1930s and 1940s when Japan overshadowed Chinese national integrity, and as in the 1950s and 1960s when, at least in Chinese eyes, the United States seemed to challenge China's territorial integrity (this time at the Yalu and later at the Red River Delta), China's national independence ha: been consistently challenged. By the late 1960s China's newest rival had become the Soviet Union. As recently as 1969 there was open warfare between the two countries on the Mongolian border.

Sino—Soviet Rivalry

Although there has been a marked improvement in relations between the two Communist superpowers since 1969, most notably in the form of a trade agreement and the exchange of ambassadors, the underlying clash of ideological and national interests remains. Meanwhile, in the last few years, following the British withdrawal from East of Suez, which was in turn followed by the enunciation of the Nixon Doctrine promising far more limited U.S. commitment in Asia, the way has been made clear for an extension of Soviet influence in Asia. Ever since 1966 when the Soviet Union mediated between India and Pakistan over Kashmir, the Soviet Union has pursued an increasingly active role in the Indian sub-continent. This has taken the form of increasing trade, aid and technical assistance (including military hardware) and latterly a naval presence in the Indian Ocean. Since the mid-60s the Soviet Union has gone on to cultivate closer relations with Malaysia, Singapore, the Philippines, Thailand and Indonesia. However, it is with India that the Soviet Union has established her closest partnership. In all of this it is fairly transparent that the Soviet Union is seeking to outflank and contain any future extension of Chinese influence in Asia. Moscow's proposals for an Asian collective security system, mooted in 1969, would tend to reinforce such a view. What is clear is that Soviet and Chinese rivalry already extends throughout Asia. Furthermore, Chinese trade policy is an integral element in that struggle.

China's Asian Strategy

During the Cultural Revolution of the 1960s when China concentrated on the reform of its internal social system, there was an almost complete absence of Chinese diplomatic activity in Asia. During this period China suffered a serious decline in influence. However, in the spring of 1969, Lin Pao announced a freshly formulated foreign policy. It contained two quite separate policies to suit two quite distinct groups of countries. Both of these twin policies are still being pursued by China today.

The first of these policies was a classic Marxist foreign policy of backing the people's liberation struggles. This was the policy China chose to pursue in India, Indonesia, Malaysia, Singapore, the Philippines, Thailand and Burma. It is noticeable that in each of these countries with the possible exceptions of Thailand and Burma, China has very little common cause with the governments in power, either ideologically or in terms of practical politics. Moreover, it should be noted that these are the very same countries and governments which the Soviet Union has begun to assiduously cultivate, not without some success.

The second of Lin Pao's twin policies in Asia is known as the diplomacy of Five Peace Principles. This is the policy which governs China's relations with Pakistan, North Korea, North Vietnam, Cambodia, Laos, Nepal, Tibet and Afghanistan, which embraces an area which China has begun to tacitly regard as her own particular sphere of influence. With the sole exception of Pakistan, each of these countries constitutes a traditional area of Chinese influence. They also constitute buffer zones, North Korea, Indo-China and the 'northern tier' of Afghanistan, Nepal and Tibet forming a semi-circle of client states on China's southern underbelly.

China's World-wide Market Diversification

Since the de-escalation of the Vietnam war, and the 'solution' of the problem of Formosa, the path has been cleared for China to extend her world-wide diplomatic role, not simply at international organisations such as the United Nations, but by an expanded series of bilateral relations. Holding firmly to her belief in not developing any exclusive relationship with any single major power, or even region, China has managed to distribute her overseas trade about equally to five major trading regions. They are Japan (25 per cent), Eastern Europe (20 per cent), Western Europe and North America (20 per cent), the Third World (20 per cent) and the great Far Eastern free ports, Hong Kong and Singapore (15 per cent). With both Japan and Eastern Europe, China has imported machinery and capital goods, providing them in return with raw materials and foodstuffs; in the case of Western Europe and North America, China has been seeking advanced technological products, such as aircraft, in return for foodstuffs and light manufactures. With the Third World, with whom it has been an article of faith to trade with, China has been buying growing quantities of raw materials. By the end of the decade China plans to be importing more than 30 per cent of her imports from Third

World countries. If one doubts the influence of ideology on the direction of trade, a short survey of China's Third World trade partners should confirm its importance. China's leading trade partners in Latin America, at least until 1973, were Chile and Peru (from whom she imported copper, lead, zinc, fishmeal, etc.); in Africa they are Algeria and Tanzania (mostly phosphates and sulphur), though recently Nigeria has crept up; in the Middle East China's trade partners include Iraq, the Sudan, Egypt and Syria.

Eastern European Trade

In the 1950s, as we have noted, China's external trade was almost exclusively with the Soviet bloc. After the ideological split much of this trade, which amounted to about 80 per cent of China's total trade, was diverted to Japan and Western Europe. However, her trade with Eastern Europe is beginning to pick up again. China's chief trading partners, in order of importance, Albania, Romania, Poland and Bulgaria, reflect fairly accurately the degree of ideological sympathy with Peking. However, the most striking new trade partner China has developed in Europe, which may or may not have some ideological significance, has been Yugoslavia, with whom China has ordered an increasing number of ships. Indeed, like her arch rival, the Soviet Union, China has been systematically building a very powerful merchant marine which already numbers about 400 ships. At the moment the China National Machinery Import and Export Corporation has orders for around 200,000 tons of new shipping being built abroad, chiefly in Romania, Yugoslavia and of course Japan. Apart from ships, China's main imports from Eastern Europe are goods such as non-ferrous metals and pharmaceuticals. In return China exports resin, paper, tin, tung oil and textiles.

Sino—Japanese Trade

For some time China's most important trading partner has been Japan. With the restoration of full diplomatic relations in September 1972, trade has continued to expand steadily. Although China's trade with Japan was worth around £330 million in 1972, which may not seem much in Western terms (or Japanese terms for that matter), it represented an increase of nearly 25 per cent in 1971. The outlook promises a rapid expansion, not least because Japan needs ever increasing supplies of oil.

With a crude oil output in excess of forty million tons, much of it from the newly developed Taching oilfield, China has already agreed to provide one million tons annually to Japan with every indication that this will eventually become a significant source of Japan's future oil supplies. China also exports soyabeans, seafoods, silk, salt and chestnuts to Japan. In return she imports from Japan mostly steel products of one kind or another.

Western Europe and North America

Until very recently it was illegal to trade with China if you were an American citizen. Not surprisingly China's trade with the United States is still not very substantial but, like Western Europe, it possesses an advanced technology which China is anxious to buy. The most obvious example of this is China's interest in purchasing commercial aircraft such as the Anglo—French Concorde, the British Trident and the American Boeing 707. Among West European countries Britain has been a traditional trading partner; if after Japan one counts Hong Kong (still a British colony) as the second most important trading partner, Germany would come third and France not far behind. In the case of Anglo—Chinese trade, there is the restriction of British quantitive controls, which saw the volume of trade transacted between the two countries decline in 1972 compared with the later 1960s. Moreover, since 20 per cent of China's exports to Britain have been farm or fish products the EEC's Common Agricultural Policy will adversely affect Anglo—Chinese trade. China's manufactures in glassware, footwear, etc., will also be restricted by the Common External Tariff of the European Community, though this is likely to be partially compensated for by a reduction of quantitive controls as British and EEC trade policies are harmonised.

Conclusion

Any attempt to encapsulate the entire range of China's economic foreign policy would be self-defeating if only because it is both wide-ranging and, for an ideologically motivated nation, relatively flexible. However, there are several discernible strands which stand out. First, since China remains uniquely self-sufficient among the world's great powers her economic impact is proportionately restricted and is of necessity more cautious. Thus her export–import pattern with each country is closely balanced. Secondly, pursuing a world-wide market diversification strategy China has to date distributed her trade about equally with five major regions, namely Japan, Eastern Europe, Western Europe, North America, the Third World, and finally the great Far Eastern ports of Hong Kong and Singapore. Thirdly, as the Soviet Union's great rival in Asia, China is pursuing twin Asian policies of either revolution or diplomacy according to whether the country is sympathetic to Moscow or Peking. Fourthly, as part and parcel of her championing the interests of the Third World, China's trade with Third World countries is growing at a relatively faster rate than with any other group of nations, especially with Asia and Latin America. Much of this growth is at the expense of Western Europe. Now that Britain has adopted the EEC's Common Agricultural Policy and Common External Tariff the likelihood is that China will be unable to export as much as she would wish to Britain. Since China's policy is to balance her trade, not only will much of these traditional exports to Britain be diverted to the Third World but in turn China will take more of their imports. To some extent there is a real possibility that China will replace Britain as one of the great bridging nations between the industrialised and non-industrialised world. There is little doubt it is China's aim.

Conclusion: The Shadow of the Superblocs

The conflict of the superblocs is virtually a post-ideological or at least a supra-ideological conflict born out of economic trends. These trends have their antecedents in economic nationalism which has been enlarged by demographic factors. Thus the combination of substantial populations and enormous productive capacity (and in the case of the United States and the Soviet Union colossal military capacity) have made the United States, the Soviet Union, the EEC, Japan and China colossi whose economic tentacles embrace practically the entire globe. The conflicts which exist between them are as much the fruit of their different historical experience as of any specifically ideological differences as the intensity of the rivalry between the two specifically Communist colossi amply illustrates. As each superbloc stakes out its sphere of influence there is a major area whose control is likely to be bitterly disputed. The Middle East, because of its oil and its strategically pre-eminent location, is a region where the superblocs are likely to clash even without the existence of the historically intransigent differences between the Arabs and Israel. The detente between the superpowers can demonstrably be threatened in the space of a few days by events in the area. Moreover, the ambivalent attitudes of the elements which make up the European Community towards the Arabs and the Israelis respectively also pose special problems.

Indeed, since by its very nature a superbloc is always jostling its neighbouring superbloc in order to avoid fragmentation of its economic satellites, conflict between a French–dominated EEC with largely pro–Arab sympathies and a United States with its ethnic, cultural and traditional support of Israel is virtually inescapable. Such a conflict is likely to be

79

both compounded and complicated by such factors as oil and migrant labour, characteristic requirements of the expanding superbloc. As in conventional wars, once an economic war has broken out the conflict becomes a bitter propaganda battle in which each superbloc deploys highly selective accounts of the issues as stake — which is a further reason for weighing up the global effects of any major policy before it is introduced and has subsequently to be justified regardless of whose vital interests it infringes.

Third World Goals

World trade grew in value in 1972 by 17 per cent thanks to a growth in the volume of trade of 10 per cent. Trade by the developed countries, however, grew in *value* substantially faster in percentage terms than those of the developing countries in spite of the fact that in *volume* terms the positions were reversed. In plain language this means that in 1972 the Third World's terms of trade continued to decline. With the exception of oil, whose scarcity is likely to be permanently guaranteed from now on, the recent temporary boom in commodity prices has tended to give a more favourable gloss to the relative position of the Third World. Which brings us face to face with one of the central questions of the decade. Will the enlargement of the EEC benefit the Third World either directly, through increased aid, or indirectly, through enlarged trading opportunities?

First, disposing of aid. On all the evidence available the effects of all aid programmes suggest that their cumulative effects are mostly marginal — up to this moment at least. Whether this is a commentary on the nature of aid and where it was deployed, and how, or merely a commentary on the principle of aid (i.e. non-emergency aid), a simple increase in the volume of aid as we have known it will contribute very little to closing the gap between the rich and the poor world-wide.

Secondly, the question of export markets. Bearing in mind that Sir Christopher Soames, the EEC's External Trade Commissioner, has made considerable play of the fact that the enlarged Community is the largest trading bloc in the world it is logical to examine its overall effect on the Third World. When the EEC was first conceived it represented above all else a practical means of burying the hatchet of Franco—German rivalry which had spawned three terrible wars in less than a century. It was the dream of creating a post-national society. To some extent this dream has been realised. Nobody expects France or Germany to embark on any military adventures against the other. The Rhine, for instance, has come to be regarded merely as a great commercial waterway and tourist attraction. The fault lines of the world we inhabit lie elsewhere, as Barbara Ward felicitously pointed out some time ago. Today the great divide is of course between the industrialised north and the non-industrialised south. It is important to remember that when the Treaty of Rome was drawn up this awareness did not exist. To a large extent the EEC has so far failed to adapt to this enormous challenge. It is not simply a question of subsidising domestic sugar and rice producers but the overall trend of the EEC towards agricultural self-sufficiency. The final effect of such a trend would be to deprive the Third World of the very opportunity which offers most hope — guaranteed agricultural (and to a lesser extent manufactures) export markets.

There has been a vast amount written about the external policies of the EEC in relation to the Third World and a great deal of play has been made of the various concessions and special arrangements. Many of these arrangements represent genuine concessions to the interests of Third World countries and reflect an honest effort on the part of the negotiators to reconcile the interests of the EEC producers and those of the Third World. Nevertheless the overall effect of this massive series of special arrangements is to serve as a smokescreen for the total impact of the Community on the Third World which can only be described as generally adverse and frequently discriminatory. A few overall statistics make this point very plain.

First, assuming all those countries who are eligible for association under a renegotiated Yaoundé Convention agreement become associates they will represent a mere 12 per cent of the population of the Third World. Furthermore, the very terms of association are likely to create a minority of mainly French and to a lesser extent ex-British colonies who will constitute a privileged minority within the Third World. Secondly, to those Third World countries who are ineligible for association, for whom trade in raw materials, processed agricultural goods and certain manufactures is absolutely vital, the EEC operates a rigorously protectionist Common Agricultural Policy whose world-wide effects we have already glimpsed. But the practical effects are even worse than the tariffs against raw commodities might suggest.

Taking the example of cocoa, although the tariff on cocoa beans is only 3.2 per cent that on the processed product of cocoa powder is 18.2 per cent. Since the value added to cocoa by the process is only 12 per cent the levy of a further 15 per cent tariff on the processed product effectively prevents its processing outside Europe. In effect the EEC is prepared to impose a tariff against Third World processors of around 140 per cent in the case of cocoa. Further examples could be multiplied. The significance of these tariffs is that they undermine market stability and remove any possibility of obtaining reasonable profit margins for the producers.

A similar situation prevails in the tariffs against Third World manufactured exports. In July 1971, to the accompaniment of considerable fanfare, the EEC introduced its Generalised Scheme of Preference to 'encourage' the export of manufactured goods from non-associated Third World countries. To date this scheme covers precisely 7 per cent of exports from the Third World to the EEC and specifically discriminates against many manufactures, notably textile and leather goods. In 1972, for instance, the Common External Tariff was re-imposed on Third World textile products no less than thirty-five times. The situation is aptly summed up in the stark statistic that the average effective tariff imposed by the EEC on *all* industrial imports was 11.1 per cent in 1972 whereas the average effective tariff imposed on industrial imports from the Third World was 16.9 per cent.

To lend some perspective to these figures it is useful to remind oneself that this Third World, which the industrialised world has successfully subordinated to serve its own growth until now, is beginning to flex its muscles in the case of the oil-producing countries. It cannot be long before the producers of other scarce commodities will discover unforeseen strength when they combine together. None of this newly discovered bargaining strength should disguise the fact that the vast majority if the Third World is underfed and that the Third World, comprising the majority of mankind, notwithstanding the boom in oil prices and certain scarce commodities, remains desperately poor. It is against this section of the world's people that Europe, once the greatest coloniser the world has seen, now the greatest single influence on world trade, must exercise the greatest sense of responsibility in the interests of everyone. The legacy of colonialism is not simply one of tied economies but also of inherited theories of development which by reinforcing self-perpetuating élites (e.g. the university educated who have staffed the upper echelons of the civil service without the restraints imposed by other concentrations of the highly educated) have often retarded the long-term economic and social development of the county concerned. Rather than investing in agriculture, which would have maximised wealth for the greatest possible number, the European trained élites concentrated on Western-style education and industrialisation with a consequent polarisation of wealth and an increasingly apparent maldistribution of resources. In short, the Third World has suffered not only from adverse external trading arrangements, especially with Europe, but also inappropriate internal development practices, chiefly adopted from Europe. In the former instance the opportunity for amendment is still there.

Within the span of this book it is only possible to hint at some of the overall trends which seem to be taking place within the world economic system. In compiling such a brief survey it is not intended to suggest that the trends all point in a single direction. Indeed, there has been a remarkable growth in the world economy during the last fifteen years. It would be foolish however to assume that this will continue as a matter of course. It would be even more foolish to ignore the signs of political and economic conflict when they appear. Far better to face such differences squarely rather than wishing they would go away.

If a single overall conclusion must be drawn from this book it is that the world is moving towards a five-power regional economic or superbloc system. Having recognised that this is already taking place the next step is to see *how* it is taking place. At the moment there is a considerable element of regionalism at the expense of world-wide interests. To combat this trend this book puts forward a skeleton six-point programme of priorities which need to be tackled if the drift into protectionism is to be halted.*

(1) *Agriculture.* One of the features which becomes quite clear from a survey of this kind is the world-wide and generally adverse effects of the Common Agricultural Policy designed to make Western Europe self-sufficient in agriculture. The CAP needs to be reformed. This would have to incorporate such measures as limitation of export subsidies, restriction of export restitution, introduction of certificates of value for dairy farmers and a reduction of threshold price levels for cereal farmers who would be compensated by direct payments based on past acreage, etc. If the CAP is not reformed then it will have to be dismantled. If the French maintain their position that the CAP is 'non-negotiable' then a trade war is a virtual certainty.

(2) *Third World Guarantees.* Bearing in mind that agricultural commodities represent the primary source of the Third World's income they need above all else guaranteed access and guaranteed prices for their primary exports. In addition they need more development finance through untied agencies who will invest in the agricultural sector rather than the generally more profitable industrial sector. Whether this should involve a link with the IMF's special drawing rights is arguable. At the moment the preferences offered by the developed world are derisory. The EEC's association agreement, for instance, would cover only about 12 per cent of the Third World's population if all those to whom it is being offered became associates.

(3) *Multinationals and Non-Tariff Barriers.* While on balance the role of the multinational companies has been

*A comprehensive set of proposals on trade liberalisation is to be found in *Towards An Open World Economy* (Frank McFadzean *et al.*) Macmillan, 1972.

generally beneficial there is a need for international rules of conduct for organisations deploying such vast manpower and financial resources. Again, while non-tariff barriers have begun to be listed as they become more significant than tariff barriers, they also need some code or agency which will exercise some form of restraint on behalf of maintaining an open world trading system.

(4) *Fixed but Adjustable Exchange Rates.* As has been pointed out in the section on the monetary challenge, the present system has unofficially evolved into one of frequent changes in exchange rates (sometimes from floating, sometimes not) in response to market forces. The ideal practical objective would be to so reinforce the International Monetary Fund that it could police a monetary system to meet the needs of the world trading system. Such a system would include an agreed formula for deciding when any country's official reserves registered disproportionate changes requiring an adjustment in the exchange rate, either up or down.

(5) *Role of the Special Drawing Rights.* Assuming that SDRs will play an increasingly important role in the reserve system their particular function in the sphere of development assistance needs to be clearly defined. In order not to overload an as yet unproven reserve *numéraire* or counter SDRs should be regarded as reserve credits made available to developing countries *in addition* to their normal sources of external aid. By introducing extra SDRs as an extra-aid programme the International Monetary Fund could maintain strict control of such credits in the interests of both the recipients and the world monetary system as a whole.

(6) *A World Energy Authority.* The establishment of a worldwide agency along the lines of GATT would bring all countries into the debate about the conservation and apportionment of scarce energy resources, on a permanent inter-government footing. A WEA should be debated in the current GATT talks and possibly launched under its aegis.

Appendix 1: Monetary Reform

By 1971 the cumulative effects of continued U.S. balance of payments deficits, an overvalued dollar, and growing foreign demand for scarce dollar reserves, began to make the role of the dollar as an international reserve currency more and more untenable. In August 1971 the United States was obliged to suspend the convertibility of the dollar. After a period of floating, a new but visibly temporary structure of fixed exchange rates was agreed in December by the Group of Ten. The Bretton Woods system could never be the same again. How different the new system will eventually become is not yet clear. What is clear is that the stability of the international monetary system, conspicuously lacking since August 1971, is an indispensable element in world trade. Should the volume of world trade slow down appreciably in the 1970s then the present exchange rate distortions could aggravate any protectionist tendencies arising from a lack of confidence in the international economic system. While there are grounds for believing a just and broadly efficient 'fixed but adjustable' exchange rate system is achievable some time in 1974 there is no room for complacency until such a goal has actually been achieved.

In the preliminary IMF executive directors' report on the reform of the international monetary system (presented in August 1972) five aspects of the international monetary system were listed as being in need of some form of overhaul.

(1) Exchange rate mechanisms. What are the precise indicators that changes in par values are necessary and what are the responsibilities of the deficit and surplus countries?

(2) Re-establishment of convertibility and the arrangements for settlement of imbalances among countries.

(3) The role of special reserve assets, namely foreign exchange reserves, gold and special drawing rights.

(4) The problem of disequilibrating capital movements and means to lessen market presures.

(5) New provisions in IMF arrangements to meet needs of developing countries.

As the Bank for International Settlements Annual Report (June 1973) points out in its *Survey of Economic Developments and Policies, 1972–73* (pp. 32–3), if it is assumed that the chief aim of reform is to re-establish a par value system with more effective adjustment incentives then the second topic, the convertibility of currencies and the methods of settling imbalances is the primary task for reform by the Committee of Twenty. It seems to be generally accepted that a return to a fixed exchange rate system is desirable but with much greater flexibility than in the past. However, as the BIS Report points out (ibid.) from 1967 to 1972 there were major exchange rate changes:

> From November 1967 until the time when the Committee (of 20) began its work, there had been eleven adjustments of fixed parities by the Group of Ten countries. There had been major devaluations of sterling, the French franc and the dollar, as well as minor ones of the lira and the Swedish krona; and all the other Group of Ten currencies, except the Canadian dollar, had been revalued, the Deutsche Mark twice. In addition, the Canadian dollar had been floating since June 1970, the Deutsche Mark and the guilder between May and December 1971, all the Group of Ten currencies between August and December 1971, and sterling from June 1972 onwards. This increased flexibility was not due to any improvement in the rules . . . . but was on the contrary both unduly delayed and set in motion by market forces.

The major question at issue in reform of the system is not so much whether greater flexibility is desirable, it has become an international fact of life, but with speeding up adjustment decisions by early identification. The main proposal here has been put forward by the United States. She proposes that 'disproportionate' changes over a given time in a country's official monetary reserves should be taken as an 'objective indicator' of the existence of a payments disequilibrium requiring corrective action. An important feature of this proposal is that it need not involve a correction in the exchange rate if a correction can be achieved by other means.

Behind this proposal are a number of principles for a reformed monetary system which have gained widespread support. They include (1) the idea that the system should make it possible for all currencies, including the dollar, to maintain convertibility into the basic reserve assets of gold and SDRs by assuming that losses of reserves can be recouped; (2) to prevent exaggerated increases in foreign exchange reserves; (3) the future growth of official reserves to be carried out chiefly through the expansion of SDR's (under international control and limited to the global needs of the system). Such a system requires that both deficit and surplus countries maintain discipline to keep changes in reserves in line with set limits or to adjust quickly to reverse excessive movements.

An alternative system to the U.S. proposal is that rather than using official reserves as the indicator, the balance of payments (allowing for the business cycle) is a more realistic gauge. Whatever system is introduced it is certain it will need to be applied with considerable flexibility until its accuracy is proven.

The French position on the key issues in any reform of the international monetary system has been spelled out, at least in outline, by the French Finance Minister, M. Valéry Giscard d'Estaing. They include three principles: (1) A return to a fixed parity system policed by a greatly reinforced International Monetary Fund; (2) the submitting of the creation of international liquidities to an effective international control; (3) the choice of a *numéraire* — a unit of reference and instrument of payments and reserve — likely to provide the widest possible confidence in the system. Indeed, it is the role and nature of reserves that provide the greatest differences of opinion, notably over the respective roles of gold and SDRs.

Given that a fixed rate system assumes the existence of reserve assets there is a growing belief that future reserves should be closely controlled to meet the demands of the world system. This emphasis on the need for control arises from a belief that excessive reserve growth leads to inflation and reflects inadequate adjustment policies. It is also widely accepted that SDR's should be the major means of reserve growth. Where there is room for disagreement is the rate of interest to be earned on SDRs and whether they should be made more independent by cutting the links with gold.

Gold itself is possibly the most controversial issue of all. At the moment gold is virtually frozen. With the market price at around $100 compared with $42 as its legal value, no central bank will surrender its gold reserves. Moreover, many countries will be loath to expand their SDRs as long as they are linked with gold-guaranteed claims on the IMF, for similar reasons as the central banks wish to hold onto their 'pure' gold reserves.*

If the international monetary system is to serve the needs of the global community with the maximum flexibility within a fixed system it seems desirable that the importance of SDRs will increase at the expense of gold. Whether gold should be phased out completely, and if so how; whether it should be retained with very little alteration and whether it should maintain its link with the SDRs; whether the fixed official value should be ignored, leaving gold-holding countries to employ it in settlements at the market price — the most likely possibility — or whether gold should remain much as it is, all these remain hotly debated questions.

Finally, the method of discriminating in favour of the developing countries through a reformed international monetary system has not yet been fully thought out. The concept of the 'link' between SDRs and development aid whereby developing countries would be allocated more than their share of SDRs needs close scrutiny.

In monetary terms, it raises serious difficulties. SDRs were not invented to finance persistent deficits and if their share of SDRs grew very rapidly it could very readily undermine confidence in the system. If a link were introduced would it prove more efficient than conventional aid? The answers to these questions are far from clear.

*Gold currently represents only about 15 per cent of the $121,000 m. of industrialised countries' total reserves, though the possibility of the major Arab oil states converting their dollar holdings of about $10,000 m. into gold cannot be discounted.

Appendix 2: Britain, the EEC and Britain's Overseas Trade*

After ten years of concentrating on entry to the EEC it is especially important to remember that, even in 1972, more than half of Britain's overseas visible and invisible trade lay outside Western Europe. Moreover, that Britain's competitiveness in the past has been based on importing cheap food and raw materials and in return exporting manufactured goods to the same trading partners. Furthermore, that the provision of capital and services has not only helped to put Britain's overseas payments in surplus but has been an integral element in the retention of many of her most lucrative export markets. Thus in the period 1961—71 British 'invisible' trade with the Commonwealth and Sterling Area doubled; and at the end of the same period total British visible and invisible trade with the Commonwealth and Sterling Area still exceeded that with the EEC. However, latterly the pattern of British direct investment overseas has noticeably begun to change. Thus in 1971 direct investment in the EEC rose from £71 million (in 1970) to £244m., while investment in the Sterling Area fell from £222m. (in 1970) to £182m. Following the Commons vote approving entry in October 1971 there has been an even more pronounced switch of British trade and investment towards the EEC during 1972. Indeed, in the twelve months following October 1971 British exports to the EEC rose by £250m. while her exports to the Commonwealth fell by £159m.

In 1967 Britain's four main trading partners were the

*As the main part of the book demonstrates the worldwide effects of the EEC and suggests that the entry of Britain will accelerate these trends, this appendix documents and analyses the trends in British overseas trade since membership of the EEC became a major economic objective.

Sterling Area (30 per cent), the EEC (19 per cent), North America (18 per cent) and EFTA (15 per cent), leaving only 18 per cent with all Britain's remaining trading partners. By January 1973 Britain's four main trading partners were the same groups but radically altered in their respective import- ance. Although the Sterling Area remained marginally (£17 m.) the most important trading partner (i.e. in volume of trade transacted) the EEC accounted for the same percentage (25 per cent) of Britain's overseas trade. They were followed by EFTA (20 per cent), North America (16 per cent) and all remaining countries a meagre 14 per cent. Thus the fundamental change which has taken place in the last five years is that the EEC has, at least in percentage terms, drawn level with the Sterling Area in volume of trade transacted. It should be noted, however, that whereas Commonwealth and Sterling Area trade, taking invisibles into account, has generally provided a substantial credit balance for Britain, in 1972 Britain bought 25 per cent of her imports from the EEC but sold only 23 per cent of her exports to the Community. In absolute terms of value the imbalance was something of the order of £500 m. in 1972. By the end of 1973 Britain's visible trade deficit with her EEC partners looked like topping £1,000 m. (approx. estimate).

Thanks to an overall surplus of £660 m. in invisibles Britain was only £40 m. in overall deficit on her current account in 1972. Nevertheless, for whatever cause, the fact remains that in 1972, in the course of an increased trade and investment drive towards Europe (and in spite of a 10 per cent devaluation of sterling from floating) Britain dissipated a £1,042 m. trade surplus achieved during 1971. By the begin- ning of 1974 Britain's payments deficit was around £2,000 m. (approx. estimate), or about 4 per cent of the national income, despite a further 10 per cent downward float of sterling during 1973. Furthermore, Britain's trade is relatively more significant as a barometer of the country's economic prosperity than that of most major industrialised countries because of the very high percentage of her GNP represented by her external trade, around four times that of the United States and almost double that of Japan. Hence Britain's interest in maintaining the maximum freedom in world trading conditions is considerably greater than that of most industrialised countries.

A preliminary comparison of the value of British exports to selected areas in 1963 and 1972 gives some idea of the trends in British external trade during a period when Britain was increasingly preoccupied with obtaining entry into the EEC. In the early 1960s Britain resolutely sought to preserve her Commonwealth and world-wide trading system; latterly she has been much less concerned about their preservation. These underlying political factors should be borne in mind in surveying Table 1 below.

Table 1   Value of British exports and imports: an analysis
by destination and source

£1 million

	Exports		Imports	
Sterling Area	*1963*	*1972*	*1963*	*1972*
Sterling Area	1,408	2,376	1,750	2,600
North America	583	1,598	883	1,785
Western Europe	1,656	4,177	1,512	4,900
EEC	940	2,230	790	2,729
EFTA	574	1,587	609	1,961
Eastern Europe	134	275	178	396
Latin America	144	338	299	329
Rest of World	336	948	360	1,125
Total vis. trade	4,365	9,746	4,983	11,155
Total deficit	£1,409m.			

Table 1 reveals a number of trends which have taken place during the last ten years, most of which will be examined later on in this appendix. One feature, however, stands out. Ten years ago 30 per cent of British trade was carried out with Western Europe, now it is around 45 per cent, an important verification of a deliberate pursuit by the British Government of an increasingly Eurocentric trade pattern. Nevertheless the value of British exports to the Sterling Area in 1972 (£2,376 m.) still exceeded British exports to the EEC (£2,230 m.) by a comfortable margin of £146 m., leaving the Sterling Area Britain's most important export market in 1972 even without taking account of Britain's substantial invisible surplus with the Commonwealth.

Altogether, Britain's major export markets in 1972 in order of importance were the Sterling Area (24 per cent), the EEC (23 per cent), North America (16 per cent) and EFTA (16 per cent), with all other export markets accounting for a total of 21 per cent. Taking Western Europe as a whole, we find it purchased 40 per cent of all British exports in 1972, valued at £4,200 m. However, since Britain imported £4,900 m. worth of goods from Western Europe it had a trade deficit with Europe of £700 m. (compared with around £200 m. with the Sterling Area which was more than compensated for by invisibles). If Anglo-EEC trade expands at the present rate (16 per cent in 1972, though the British share in the EEC market has not increased for some years) and the imbalance expands by the same proportions, Britain will be facing a severe balance of payments crisis unless she maintains and expands her non-European trading links. That option is still to some extent open to us as can be seen if we examine the destination of total British exports. Thus putting the spectacular growth of the EEC and European markets in 1972 into perspective, 77 per cent of all British exports went to non-EEC destinations, while 60 per cent was exported to countries outside Western Europe. As Britain progressively adopts more and more EEC policies affecting her world-wide trade, from the Common External Tariff to the Common Agricultural Policy, and as its Commonwealth partners terminate their preferences for British goods, it will become ever more important to maintain and diversify British trade outlets. Britain's competitiveness in the West European market looks sufficiently suspect at this stage to make the maintenance of world-wide trading outlets imperative.

British External Trade Trends, 1963–72

As we have already seen, in the ten years preceding entry into the EEC the pattern of Britain's external trade has undergone a profound change. The following section examines trends in the destination of British exports and the source of British imports in greater detail.

The Sterling Area

In 1963 the Sterling Area accounted for about one-third of the total value of Britain's external trade; by 1972 it had shrunk in relative importance to a quarter. The Sterling Area (exclusive of Britain) then, as now, comprises around six developed nations and a majority group of around twenty plus developing nations. In 1963 almost 50 per cent of British Sterling Area exports went to the four most important developed countries, that is to Australia, South Africa, Ireland and New Zealand (or around £720 m.). By 1972 the volume of British exports to the big four had doubled to £1,240 m. or more than 75 per cent of all British exports to the Sterling Area (i.e. £1,600 m.). Among the developing countries in 1972 only Nigeria (£154 m.), India (£141 m.) and Hong Kong (£101 m.) constituted export markets for Britain in excess of £100 m. Several others, such as Bahrein and Kuwait (£94 m.), Singapore (£77 m.), Malaysia (£62 m.), Kenya (£55 m.), Libya (£46 m.) and Zambia (£46 m.), remain rich in potential.

Meanwhile, in the same period, British imports from the Sterling Area have grown much more rapidly, from £1,750 m. to £2,600 m. Among the big four, British imports grew from £705 m. to £1,273 m. and although Ireland recorded by far the most spectacular increase and accounted for nearly a third of total British imports from the four in 1972 nevertheless South Africa, Australia and New Zealand each recorded increases. In 1963 British imports from the big four represented 40 per cent of imports from the Sterling Area; by 1972 it had reached 50 per cent. Only five of the developing countries exported goods in excess of £100 m. in 1972. They included Bahrein and Kuwait (£278 m.), Hong Kong (£184 m.), Nigeria (£156 m.), Libya (£144 m.) and India (£112 m.), of whom all except Hong Kong and India derived nearly all their export earnings from petroleum. Yet if the total value of goods imported from the vast majority of developing countries in the Sterling Area seems small it nevertheless represents for most of them, the single most important export market.

North America

Although British exports to North America were about half the value of those to the Sterling Area in 1963, ten years later British exports to North America had almost tripled in value to £1,598 m. while imports had merely doubled to £1,785 m. Taking them separately, Britain more than doubled the value of her exports to Canada, worth £180 m. in 1963 and £380 m. in 1972, while Canadian exports to Britain grew from £374 m. in 1963 to £605 m. in 1972.

In the same ten-year period British exports to the U.S. tripled while imports more than doubled. Thus in 1972 British exports to the U.S. reached £1,207 m., exceeding imports (at £1,171 m.) for the first time for many years. However, Britain had a total visible trade deficit with North America in 1972 of about £200 m.

Western Europe

The overall growth of Anglo-European trade is, as we have noted, the most striking development in Britain's overseas trade during the last ten years. Britain's trading partners in Western Europe have comprised three distinct groups – the EEC (six members), EFTA (seven members) and four others, Greece, Turkey, Yugoslavia and Spain. Britain's trade with the EEC represents by far the most important of these three. As a member of EFTA and non-member of the EEC during this period Britain has unsurprisingly registered the most spectacular growth in trade with her then partners in EFTA, rather than the Six. Thus Britain's exports to EFTA countries tripled in value from £574 m. in 1963 to £1,587 m. in 1972, as did imports which grew from £609 m. in 1963 to £1,961 m. in 1972. Even so the value of British exports to the EEC in 1972 at £2,230 m. exceeded its exports to EFTA by around £640 m. The most spectacular increases in British exports to the EEC in the last ten years were to West Germany (which more than doubled and increased in absolute terms by £348 m.) and France (again more than doubled and increased by £315 m.). The increase in British imports from the same countries was even more spectacular. British imports from West Germany nearly quadrupled (an increase of £628 m.) as did those from France (an increase of £405 m.). In 1972 West Germany (£841 m.) was Britain's major source of EEC imports followed by the Netherlands (£615 m.), with France (£603 m.) a close third. The nature of this vast increase in trade is partly explained in a later section of this appendix which analyses commodity trading figures.

Of the remaining regions in the world with which Britain trades the Middle East (£754 m.) is currently by far the most important, followed by Eastern Europe (£671 m.), Latin America (£667 m.) and the Far East (£612 m.). Their respective importance as export markets is, first, the Middle East (£412 m.), followed by Latin America (£338 m.), Eastern Europe (£274 m.) and the Far East (£252 m.).

Within these four regions the major customers for British exports are Japan (£172 m.), Israel (£135 m.), Iran (£117 m.), Soviet Union (£90 m.), Brazil (£84 m.), Poland (£75 m.) and the Argentine Republic (£51 m.). The leading sources of British imports in the same areas are Japan (£313 m.), Soviet Union (£227 m.), Saudi Arabia (£184 m.), Iran (£123 m.), Brazil (£86 m.), Argentine Republic (£77 m.), Poland (£71 m.), Venezuela (£57 m.) and Israel (£57 m.). Thus Britain's four most important trading partners in the four regions are Japan (£485 m.), Soviet Union (£317 m.), Iran (£240 m.) and Saudi Arabia (£229 m.). In May 1973 the British Government announced a £250 m. defence contract between the Saudi Arabian Government and the British Aircraft Corporation. (See Table 2, 'Exports and Imports by Country and Region, 1963 and 72'.)

U.K. Commodity External Trade Trends, 1968–72

In the following section there is a brief analysis of the trends in commodities traded in by Britain during the last five years. Probably the two most significant features of the commodity trends charted at the end of this section are that, in the period examined, (1) imports of essentials such as food, raw materials and fuels increased only marginally, while imports of less essential manufactured goods such as cars, washing machines, TV sets, typewriters, etc., have spiralled. (2) Britain's traditional major exports, machinery, transport equipment, semi-manufactures, chemicals and finished manufactures are now being matched by even greater quantities of imports of the very same kinds of goods. Thus Britain is increasingly exchanging different versions of the same commodity with its trading partners. This can be seen most strikingly in machinery and transport equipment where a growth of around £700 m. in exports and £800 m. in imports from Western Europe during the last ten years reflects the virtual existence of a free trade area in engineering machinery already. Exports of manufactured goods to Western Europe also rose a not insubstantial £400 m., while imports from the same countries rose £500 m.

The underlying significance of these trends is that Britain has begun to abandon the pattern of trading with complementary economies and has now embarked increasingly to trade with broadly similar economies. This will broaden the range of choice to the consumer, it will also push out of business the marginally inefficient producer unless there is some form of public intervention.

To illustrate the two earlier points in greater detail, if we examine the trading in machinery and transport equipment, we find it accounted for around 40 per cent of all British exports over the last five years. In 1968 Britain exported £903 m. worth of machinery and transport equipment to Western Europe, substantially its largest export market for these goods. By 1972 Britain exported £1,596 m. of the same goods to Western Europe. Meanwhile, Britain, which had imported £629 m. worth of machinery and transport equipment from Western Europe in 1968, imported £1,439 m. worth in 1972. In other words, in the sector and market where Britain sold most in the past she is now buying almost as much abroad as she sells.

A second illustration is the import of food and live animals. In 1972 this amounted to almost £1,000 m. from the Sterling Area alone, a 25 per cent increase, as five years before it was £800 million. In the import of crude materials very little increase was recorded over the last five years except with Western Europe where a 25 per cent increase took place. Compare these with the percentage increases in the import of manufactured goods where the increase in Britain's trade with Western Europe was about 45 per cent. These figures, extracted from the following commodity trends charts, suggest the overall pattern of trade which has switched from the buying and selling of dissimilar goods to the buying and selling of goods of much the same type.

U.K. Commodities External Trade Summary Chart*

	Exports	1967	1972	Imports	1967	1972
major exports	1. Machinery & Transport Equipment	42%	41%		13%	20%
	2. Semi-Manufactures	25%	24%		19%	21%
	3. Chemicals	9%	10%	1–4 covers	6%	5%
				85% of 54% of		
				exports imports		
	4. Other Finished Manufactures	8%	10%		6%	8%
				5–7 covers		
major imports	5. Food, beverages, tobacco	9%	8%	15% of 46% of exports imports	28%	22%
	6. Basic Materials	5%	4%		15%	12%
	7. Mineral Fuel Lubricants	3%	3%		12%	12%

What is worth noting in the above chart, covering the last six years, is that there has been a decline in the percentage exports in the two main exporting sectors, machinery and transport equipment and semi-manufactures, matched by a substantial increase in imports in the same two categories. This may suggest that Britain has become progressively less competitive in the two sectors where more than 60 per cent of its exports traditionally originate. The chart also reveals that the percentage of food and basic materials imported noticeably declined, reflecting the relative decline in imports from the Commonwealth and Sterling Area.

(See Table 3, 'An Analysis of the Trends in Major Commodities traded in by the U.K. from 1968 to 1972'.)

*DTI Report.

Britain's Trade in Invisibles

For nearly 200 years Britain has relied on invisibles — largely earnings from shipping, insurance, banking and receipts from overseas investments — to provide a surplus on its external trade. In 1969, 68 per cent of Britain's invisible trade was with the Commonwealth and Sterling Area, North America, and EFTA, and around 16 per cent with the EEC. In the same year Britain had a total surplus in invisibles, with all countries, of £557 m., of which £339 m. came from the Sterling Area Surplus. It also had a trade deficit in invisibles with the EEC of £118 m. As with visible trade, only more so, the temptation to concentrate on the EEC at the expense of the rest of the world could impose a severe strain on Britain's balance of payments.

By 1971 Britain earned over £5,276 m. from invisibles (around 40 per cent of Britain's total foreign income), producing a net surplus of £741 m., considerably more than double the £229 m. visible trade surplus. In 1972, however, when Britain was much more strenuously redirecting her trade towards Europe, the surplus in invisibles fell by around £90 m. To illustrate, the average invisible *surplus* for the first three-quarters in 1972 was £165 m. compared with £186 m. in 1971. By comparison, the average visible trade *deficit* in the first three-quarters of 1972 was £160 m. compared with an average trade *surplus* of £111 m. for the same period in 1971. Again comparing the same periods, in 1972 there was an outflow of £899 m. in investment and other capital flows whereas in 1971 there was an inflow of £1,384 m. Or broken down a bit further, in 1972 (in the first three-quarters) there was a total of £444 m. of overseas investment in the U.K. private sector compared with £742 m. in 1971. The decline in foreign investment in Britain was matched by the growth in U.K. private investment overseas; in 1971, during the first three-quarters, it was £598 m.; the same period in 1972, £970 m. Put differently, in 1972 there was twice as much U.K. private capital going abroad as there was coming in from overseas. The significance of this is far more long-term than the mere current balance sheet and if maintained could reflect a serious weakness in Britain's capacity to attract investment.

The high importance of invisibles to Britain can be seen by two different sorts of comparisons with other industrialised countries. First, in 1968 Britain accounted for 12 per cent of world invisible receipts. Apart from the United States with 25 per cent, no other country accounted for more than 6 per cent (France, Italy and West Germany each accounted for around 6 per cent in fact). Secondly, in 1968 (the latest comparative figures available) invisibles accounted for 34 per cent of British total foreign earnings, compared with 32 per cent for the United States, 29 per cent for Italy, 25 per cent for France and 14 per cent for West Germany. Among the Nine only the Benelux countries exceeded the British percentage. Clearly Britain has the most highly developed trade in invisibles of any major European country. She needs to preserve and expand that system if she is to maintain her overall competitiveness.

Note. In 1968 Britain's four major destinations for overseas capital investment were Australia, Canada, the United States and South Africa, in that order.

Conclusions

Ten years ago Britain began its switch in trading priorities from the Commonwealth to the United States and more especially to Europe. However, the Commonwealth and Sterling Area trade remained substantial for two main reasons. First, it was the most efficient producer of food which Britain needed to import, especially meat, dairy produce, fresh and canned fruit, sugar, tea, cocoa and wheat. Secondly, it was the major world supplier of many of the raw materials (including foodstuffs) on which Britain relied for maintaining her standard of living, notably jute (96% of the world's production), tea (75%), asbestos (64%), chrome (64%), tin (57%), newsprint (52%), cocoa (50%), rubber (45%), rice (44%), bauxite (40%), sugar (26%), copper (26%), lead (25%), zinc (24%) and wheat (21%). Nevertheless, over a decade these Commonwealth markets have begun to be taken over by the Japanese, the West Germans and the Americans. A major factor in this has been Britain's failure to adapt to the changed requirements of many of her traditional trading partners. Some of the blame lies with Britain's preoccupation with expanding her trade with Europe.

Meanwhile Britain has entered the EEC. It can be taken for granted that if they can no longer export to Britain freely many of her traditional trading partners will not import from Britain but from some other supplier with whom they can export in return. Thus, according to the Commonwealth Producers Association, when the Commonwealth preference system is ended it can be assumed that 'one-third of the U.K. export with Canada and Australia and half of that with New Zealand would be lost to Britain', to which must be added the loss of invisible earnings on shipping and insurance (or about one-third of the visible trade loss). Based on the 1972 trade figures this would involve a potential loss of £473 m. worth of British overseas earnings from Canada, Australia and New Zealand alone in traditional exports.

The overriding question remains a simple one. Will Britain so increase her trade with Common Market countries that this will offset her losses with the Commonwealth and preference area? First, Britain will be attempting to substantially increase her share in an industrialised market at the expense of her consistently more heavily invested industrial rivals. Secondly, it will simultaneously be surrendering its privileged access to the world's cheapest sources of both food and manufacturing raw materials. The odds in favour of Britain balancing her trade by concentrating heavily on Europe would be very slim indeed. The 1972 trade figures would tend to confirm this initial view; the 1973 figures reinforce such a view dramatically.

A clear challenge exists for Britain to develop exports in sophisticated manufactures to the Commonwealth and preference areas where she still enjoys advantages she lacks in Europe. As a general principle, it would appear from the preceding evidence that Britain's overseas earnings potential can only be fulfilled by a concentrated attempt by both government and business to maintain and expand Britain's visible and invisible trade on a world-wide scale. An exclusive concentration in any one region, however potentially lucrative, will guarantee a continued future decline in Britain's relative economic strength.

TABLE 2   Exports and imports by country and region;
summary of last ten years*

*The following is a summary chart of the value of British exports and
imports arranged by country, for the years 1963 and 1972.*

	£ million			
	Exports		Imports	
	1963	*1972*	*1963*	*1972*
1.*Sterling Area*				
Developed countries				
Australia	238.7	317.9	207.1	283.3
New Zealand	116.0	146.8	173.6	251.5
Irish Republic	157.2	469.3	159.3	444.7
Iceland	6.3	13.4	7.1	9.3
Rep. of South Africa	207.2	308.4	166.4	295.6
S.W. Africa	1.6	1.0	14.5	23.3
Developing countries				
Cyprus	15.7	32.7	10.5	21.7
Jamaica	19.7	41.5	31.8	38.6
Trinidad	24.7	36.0	38.5	19.5
India	139.5	141.2	141.5	112.2
Pakistan	42.4	35.5	28.2	34.8
Ceylon (Sri Lanka)	23.1	11.9	41.5	22.3
Malaysia	48.8	62.1	32.5	46.6
Singapore	38.6	77.3	17.0	39.5
Hong Kong	55.6	100.9	70.0	184.7
Sierra Leone	11.5	10.3	25.6	29.0
Ghana	39.0	16.5	23.4	33.1
Nigeria	66.0	153.9	78.1	156.1
Zambia		46.2		60.3
Tanzania	10.7	17.4	21.7	22.3
Kenya	30.6	55.5	19.0	29.0
Mauritius	6.6	8.1	31.8	27.0
Bahrein, Kuwait, etc.	39.8	94.5	180.2	278.0
Libya	15.8	46.3	41.7	144.1
Other Countries	124.8		189.1	
Total Sterling Area	1,479	2,244.6	1,750	2,600

*Many of the figures employed in the following sets of tables have been rounded,
especially percentages, for ease of reference. The figures are taken from DTI
publications.

TABLE 2   (*continued*)

£ *million*

	Exports		Imports	
	1963	*1972*	*1963*	*1972*
2. *North America*				
Canada	180.0	380.0	374.0	605
United States & deps	403.0	1,207.0	508.0	1,171
Total North America	583.7	1,587.0	882.0	1,776
3. *Western Europe*				
Finland	54	137	99	247
Sweden	173	405	164	513
Norway	97	190	73	219
Denmark	108	238	166	348
Switzerland &				
Lichtenstein	80	367	65	369
Portugal	32	112	22	126
Austria	29	119	20	128
Total EFTA (excl.				
Iceland)	574	1,587	609	1,961
West Germany	242	590	213	841
Netherlands	179	451	210	615
Belgium & Luxembourg	148	394	100	315
France	196	511	157	603
Italy	175	284	110	353
Total EEC	940	2,230	790	2,729
Greece	29	68	10	17
Turkey	25	60	18	17
Yugoslavia	17	43	15	22
Spain	70	170	77	138
Total Western Europe	1,656	4,177	1,512	4,900
4. *Eastern Europe*				
Soviet Union	64	90	97	227
Poland	28	75	48	71
East Germany	8	15	10	22
Hungary	7	23	7	12
Czechoslovakia	12	24	17	32
Romania	12	39	9	25
Other countries	2	9	4	6
Total Eastern Europe	134	275	178	396

TABLE 2   (*continued*)

£ million

	Exports		Imports	
	1963	*1972*	*1963*	*1972*
5. *Latin America*				
Cuba	2	17	12	5
Mexico	15	38	7	7
Colombia	10	17	4	10
Venezuela	20	43	67	57
Peru	13	13	24	14
Brazil	19	84	27	86
Chile	11	24	28	36
Bolivia	1	2	12	17
Uruguay	7	5	17	6
Argentine Republic	25	51	89	77
Total Latin America (*Note other countries included*)	144	338	299	329
6. *Middle East*				
Iraq	18	27	62	34
Iran	28	117	34	123
Israel	45	135	20	57
Egypt	33	18	9	
Saudi Arabi	10	45	13	184
Sudan	28	23	12	5
Algeria	3	34	8	23
Morocco	5	13	10	16
Total Mid. East	170	412	170	342
7. *Far East* (i.e. non-Communist)				
Thailand	15	28	5	7
China	13	32	18	35
Japan	52	172	54	313
Philippines	12	20	4	5
Total Far East	92	252	81	360

Exports (£ million)

	North America		Sterling Area		Western Europe		Rest of World	
	1968	1972	1968	1972	1968	1972	1968	1972
Total Exports	1,183	1,599	1,808	2,377	2,402	4,177	1,041	1,563
Food and Live Animals								
Total	26.9	43.1	75.7	98.6	72.1	159.7	19.5	44
Live Animals	1.3	1.3	13.8	18.0	3.4	16.3	1.6	4.6
Meat & meat preparations	(no exports)		7.0	3.6		44.6	3.1	8.6
Dairy products, eggs	0.4	0.6	4.9	6.0	3.0	7.0	1.2	1.1
Fish & fish preparations	1.4	7.8	8.0	7.1	4.8	13.1	1.1	3.0
Fruit & vegetables	1.6	3.3	6.9	9.2	8.1	15.7	2.5	7.8
Sugar, s. preparations, honey	7.3	10.8	9.4	12.6	8.3	15.2	4.4	8.0
Coffee, cocoa, tea, spices	8.9	12.3	11.8	11.8	10.6	18.4	2.9	4.2
Cereals & preparations	3.9	4.5	11.8	13.9	21.9	11.3		
Other foods	2.0	1.4	14.0	12.3	12.1	8.6	2.7	3.0
Beverages & tobacco								
Total	113.0	127.9	39.0	42.1	47.1	83.3	37.0	61.2
Beverages	112.2	126.6	24.6	29.2	39.7	66.0	28.1	44.6
Tobacco	0.8	1.3	14.4	12.9	7.4	17.3	8.9	16.6
Crude materials								
Total	35.5	29.0	27.2	33.8	133.3	209.5	29.1	39.0
Crude rubber	0.3	1.5	2.2	2.1	11.1	22.0	3.8	2.6
Textile fibres	21.8	16.0	14.6	14.8	38.1	49.9	18.7	27.5
Crude fertilisers	2.0	1.8	4.9	6.2	24.4	38.0	1.9	3.1
Crude animal & vegetable materials	11.4	2.6	5.5	4.6	59.7	5.6	4.6	1.3

TABLE 3 (continued)

Exports (£ million)

	North America 1968	North America 1972	Sterling Area 1968	Sterling Area 1972	Western Europe 1968	Western Europe 1972	Rest of World 1968	Rest of World 1972
Mineral fuels								
Total	10.8	8.2	23.8	48.2	122.6	170.8	10.6	11.5
Petroleum	10.8	7.7	22.1	46.2	105.4	154.2	10.3	11.3
Coke, coal, gas, electricity	—	0.5	1.8	2.0	17.2	16.6	0.3	0.2
Animal & vegetable oils & fats								
Total	0.6	0.6	2.7	3.0	2.8	5.5	1.3	2.0
Chemicals								
Total	47.6	87.4	202.0	256.7	238.2	426.6	119.7	191
Chemical elements	13.3	36.0	37.2	47.5	73.2	126.8	31.2	44.0
Dyeing, tanning, etc.	5.7	9.0	20.2	23.2	26.9	48.2	16.3	25.6
Essential oils, perfumes	2.1	3.0	21.2	23.9	20.5	35.2	9.9	15.4
Medicinal & pharm. materials	6.3	12.8	38.6	58.7	31.2	69.2	20.9	40.0
Plastic materials, resins	9.8	15.0	40.0	52.6	47.4	82.0	14.2	26.8
Explosives, pyrotechnics	1.3	0.6	4.8	4.8	3.4	3.2	1.9	2.0
All others	9.1	10.7	40.1	40.4	35.6	58.9	25.4	36.0

Manufactured goods								
Total	323.5	414.4	410.8	511.4	637.0	1,069	238.8	358.0
Leather, l. material	112.4	16.6	6.3	9.4	24.9	37.1	2.4	4.0
Rubber manufactures	5.3	12.8	22.3	25.8	2 6.8	47.8	7.2	10.0
Paper & paperboard	3.1	4.6	30.8	37.0	24.7	48.4	8.0	11.7
Textile yarn and fabrics, articles	43.0	66.3	102.7	116.9	119.2	197.5	44.4	64.7
Non-metallic mineral manufactures	99.4	132.9	76.4	98.0	140.5	291.1	59.9	95.5
Iron & steel	70.5	89.2	66.2	88.8	87.2	133.7	42.7	65.3
Non-ferrous metals	62.9	52.4	27.3	33.4	158.8	208.6	43.0	52.5
Other metals	26.8	38.3	78.9	98.1	55.0	99.2	31.2	54.6
Machinery & transport equipment								
Total	451.8	624.9	803.1	1,064.2	903.2	1,596.0	498.4	730.0
Machinery (non-elec.)	229.4	342.0	343.2	472.0	441.1	821.1	296.0	418.0
Electrical machinery	53.9	65.6	181.9	232.0	134.5	259.4	53.0	105.0
Transport equipment	168.6	217.4	278.1	360.2	327.6	515.5	149.4	206.0
Miscellaneous manufactured articles								
Total	140.1	223.6	146.1	219.4	193.8	387.7	58.4	95.5
Clothing	17.9	26.5	18.0	32.9	40.9	76.2	7.7	8.7
Footwear	9.8	8.5	6.1	10.7	5.7	11.0	4.6	2.0
Prof. & scientific instruments	27.6	50.3	37.4	47.1	71.4	139.3	18.6	36.7
All manufactured goods	963		1,562		1,972		915	

TABLE 3 (continued)

Imports (£ million)

	North America 1968	North America 1972	Sterling Area 1968	Sterling Area 1972	Western Europe 1968	Western Europe 1972	Rest of World 1968	Rest of World 1972
Total Imports	1,579	1,785	2,254	2,600	2,882	4,901	1,181	1,851
Food & Live Animals								
Total	191.9	242.8	785.5	960.8	510.3	620	220	280
Live animals	1.4	2.7	53.8	64.5	1.1	4.5	0.2	
Meat & meat preparations	11.0	14.5	158.4	253.2	159.4	179.2	69.6	92.8
Dairy products, eggs	6.2	14.7	112.2	143.2	71.0	86.6	10.2	10.5
Fish & fish preparations	14.4	22.6	9.0	19.3	22.2	31.4	31.3	23.0
Fruit & vegetables	27.3	29.3	132.6	143.3	138.3	184.3	48.8	75.0
Sugar, s. preparations, honey	1.3	1.3	91.3	121.2	4.1	7.0	7.7	16.2
Coffee, cocoa, tea, spices	1.1	0.5	149.4	128.2	17.6	16.6	23.8	17.0
Cereals & preparations	109.5	132.2	38.9	47.4	63.6	65.4	20.1	5.0
Other foods	18.6	9.7	39.9	3.2	32.8	17.3	9.3	2.0
Beverages & Tobacco								
Total	83.4	79.3	40.7	43.6	65.1	123.8	3.4	8.2
Beverages	0.6	1.1	15.3	20.1	59.8	111.6	0.3	0.7
Tobacco	82.8	78.2	25.4	23.5	5.3	12.2	3.1	7.5
Crude materials								
Total	213.2	253.8	289.2	271.1	350.9	430.2	286.3	280.0
Hides, skins	8.6	10.9	24.6	30.8	13.3	18.8	16.0	24.5
Oil seeds, oil nuts	11.1	24.8	19.9	10.7	3.2	11.8	7.2	3.8

Crude rubber	7.9	5.9	26.2	22.4	6.8	13.6	7.6	5.5
Wood, lumber & cork	36.0	28.7	17.9	19.9	96.0	128.1	81.2	77.0
Pulp & waste paper	32.1	48.3	8.6	11.0	110.7	109.4	4.1	3.0
Textile fibres	12.6	14.4	100.3	94.7	39.3	45.8	67.2	58.6
Crude fertilisers	15.4	14.5	11.1	8.7	18.3	19.1	18.5	17.6
Metalliferous ores	85.5	102.3	64.0	51.5	42.1	52.7	74.8	78.0
Crude animal & vegetable materials	3.7	3.8	16.6	21.4	21.2	30.4	10.0	12.0
Mineral fuel								
Total	17.3	36.0	393.6	417.7	199.7	221.3	290.9	569.0
Petroleum	15.7	10.4	392.5	404.9	195.6	200.2	277.8	552.2
Animal & Vegetable oils and fats								
Total	5.6	12.3	37.9	44	15.0	23.1	9.3	9.8
Chemicals								
Total	121.7	152	26.1	49.5	237.0	401.6	30.6	48.0
Chemical elements	52.4	75.6	13.4	25.8	92.3	146	11.9	18.0
Essential oils, perfumes	6.1	7.6	1.8	2.5	11.3	19.9	1.6	2.6
Plastic materials & resins	28.1	31.2	1.3	4.8	49.3	97	3.7	10.0
All others	35.2	50	9.6	16	84.1	137	13.6	17.4
Manufactured goods								
Total								
Leather, l. manufactures, furs	2.7	2	20.2	26.2	6.8	9.8	3.9	9.0
Wood & cork manufactures	19.2	23.9	7.7	18.6	47.8	75	21.2	24.2
Paper, paperboard, etc.	63.5	84.4	4.9	7.6	115.2	216.9	1.7	2.5
Textile yarn, fabrics & articles	21.3	32.5	74.7	92.9	113.1	206.9	22.1	37.2

TABLE 3 *(continued)*

Imports (£ million)

	North America		Sterling Area		Western Europe		Rest of World	
	1968	*1972*	*1968*	*1972*	*1968*	*1972*	*1968*	*1972*
Non-metallic mineral manufactures	11.6	16.5	172.0	165.3	81.0	244.4	73.1	145.5
Iron & steel	16.6	24.2	8.1	10.5	115.9	178.5	14.3	47.0
Non-ferrous metals	173.8	117	193.4	146.7	101.6	121.8	98.4	61.4
Other	20.5	23.1	13.5	18.8	58.7	85.8	5.6	8.5
Machinery & Transport Equipment								
Total	469.7	499.2	43.2	99.4	629.2	1,439.5	46.5	201.6
Machinery (non-elec.)	210.8	279.3	19.2	40.4	380.4	662.9	22.2	57
Electrical machinery	90.5	128.9	17.6	39.7	115.2	290.2	13.6	67.6
Transport equipment	168.4	91	6.4	15.3	133.6	486.4	10.7	77.0
Miscellaneous manufactures								
Total	94.6	148.6	113.9	199.1	208.5	432.9	47.2	111.0
Clothing	4.7	3.9	59.8	116.0	36.7	76.6	8.9	22.0
Footwear	0.2	0.5	12.0	17.2	16.1	34.6	4.5	10.0
Prof. & scientific instruments	36.9	55.2	6.6	11.1	55.8	109.6	10.8	23.8
All other manufactures	52.9	86.4	35.4	46.3	99.9	168.3	23.1	46.2

TABLE 4   Trends in U.K. direct investment earnings 1963—70

	£ million		
	1963	*1967*	*1970*
Overseas Sterling Area	213	237	356
Australia	45	62	93
Hong Kong	4	6	10
India	21	18	20
Irish Republic	10	10	10
Malaysia	21	18	34
New Zealand	7	9	14
Nigeria	6	5	15
South Africa	47	65	87
Non-Sterling Area	117	201	325
North America	65	113	140
Canada	27	41	44
United States	38	72	96
South and Central America	16	24	31
Argentine	3	3	5
Brazil	4	9	14
Western Europe	29	41	123
EFTA	7	10	21
Portugal	2	4	5
Switzerland	2	5	9
EEC	21	25	93
Belgium & Luxembourg	3	4	14
France	5	6	17
Italy	1	2	6
Netherlands	2	3	19
West Germany	12	10	36
All areas	330	438	681
of which			
Developing Countries provided	127	136	220

Against the background of spectacular increases in investment to Western Europe the above table of U.K. earnings from direct overseas investment is salutary. It reminds the reader that as late as 1970 (the latest total figures available) the Sterling Area provided substantially more earnings on capital invested than the entire non-Sterling Area put together and the earnings from the EEC were approximately a quarter those earned from the Sterling Area. Even allowing for the switch from the Sterling Area to the EEC it will be some time before any kind of parity is reached.

Appendix 3: Britain, Portugal and Southern Africa

The Anglo—Portuguese Alliance and Southern Africa

The answer most often given as to why Portugal remains entrenched in Africa long after Britain, Belgium and France have withdrawn, is the authoritarian nature of Portugal's government, which simply did not allow a popular anti-colonial movement to grow up at home. While this was an undeniably important factor there were at least two other fundamental reasons, one historical the other demographic, behind Portugal's failure to decolonise in Africa. The first of these underlying factors springs from the nature of Portuguese colonialism, namely, the policy of assimilation with the motherland.

Even before the Roman conquest the Portuguese population comprised both European and African elements. But the crucial influence was the nearly six hundred years of Islamic occupation which not only strengthened the African component of the population but by tolerating polygamy contributed to the mixing of the races first in Portugal and subsequently in the Portuguese overseas territories. This early development of multiracialism was also accompanied by a profound conviction of the absolute value of Western civilisation, which almost alone among European nations Portugal has retained. In the twentieth century Gilberto Freyre has termed miscegenation which accepts the concept of implicit Portuguese cultural superiority as 'lusotropicalism'. It is this philosophy which continues to galvanise the mind and will of Portuguese policy makers in Luanda, Lourenco Marques and Lisbon.

The second underlying reason why Portugal wages an unremitting struggle to maintain her hold on her African territories is demographic. Angola, Mozambique and Portuguese Guinea are not merely valuable appendages of the home country but taken together are considerably more populous, 13 million inhabitants compared with metropolitan Portugal's 9½ million, and potentially far wealthier in both relative and absolute terms. Per capita income in Portugal remains the lowest in Western Europe with more than a third of the adult population unable to read or write. Moreover, unlike the African territories who produce valuable cash crops and possess substantial reserves of oil, diamonds and other minerals Portugal has relatively sparse natural resources. By enabling Portugal to buy from her own colonies at extremely low fixed prices Portugal's overseas empire has effectively disguised the relative lack of economic development at home. The indispensable nature of the African territories to the Portuguese state as presently constituted was underlined by Dr Caetano himself in a speech in which he said: 'Africa is more than an area which must be exploited. Africa is for us a morally just cause and our *raison d'être* as a state. Without Africa we would be a small nation: with Africa we are a big power.' Against such a background it is hardly surprising that Portugal has been prepared to introduce a four year conscription, maintain 160,000 soldiers abroad and devote more than a third of the total national budget to defence. As Portugal's leaders see it the present Portuguese state is fighting for its life and they are almost certainly right. In such a situation Portugal needs all the allies she can possibly muster. The question arises does Britain have any 'pull' on Portugal? The answer is 'potentially' a very great deal, once she has sorted out where her priorities lie.

In economic terms Britain and the enlarged Community, which Portugal is keen to join, provide around three quarters of Portugal's total overseas earnings and a very substantial proportion of her direct foreign investment. In 1972, for instance, as Dr Caetano pointed out on his visit to London, Anglo—Portuguese trade was worth £145 m. each way. The importance of Britain's trade with Portugal was subsequently taken up in the House of Commons Mozambique debate in 1973 by Sir Alec Douglas-Home. What neither felt worth mentioning was that the £125 m. Portuguese visible exports to Britain in 1972 represented around 30 per cent of total Portuguese exports while British exports to Portugal of £111 m. represented barely 1 per cent of total U.K. exports. In the same year the Six original EEC members plus Britain accounted for very nearly 50 per cent of all Portuguese exports (from metropolitan Portugal these were mostly pearls, wine, cork and fish). This trend is likely to increase since the introduction in 1973 of mutual reductions in industrial tariffs continuing until 1977.

But the real scale of Portugal's dependence on the enlarged Community in general and Britain in particular is seen in the fact that remittances from Portuguese migrant workers in the Community amounted to £300 m. which, together with the £150 m. earned from mostly West European tourists, represented a sum in excess of total export earnings. In round figures it can be said that Portugal derives around £600 m. annually from the Nine at the very lowest estimate (there is substantial illegal immigration and presumably illegal earnings). This represents the lion's share of Portugal's overseas earnings.

In the field of direct foreign investment on which Portugal depends very heavily indeed, since she generates very little local investment because of the socio-economic structure, it is difficult to be precise over total investment figures. In 1971 U.S. direct investment in metropolitan Portugal amounted to around £300 m. followed by U.K. investment running at about £100 m. The 1972 figures for foreign investment in Portugal *including* Angola, Mozambique and Portuguese Guinea, suggest that the three largest investors in order or importance were South Africa, Britain and the United States.

South Africa's prominent investment role can partly be explained by her putting up around two thirds of the capital for the giant Cabora Bassa dam, the largest hydro-electric scheme in Africa with double the capacity of the Kariba dam and seventy per cent greater capacity than the Aswan High Dam. Much more than a dam, Cabora Bassa is regarded as the centrepiece of a great development project linking Mozambique with South Africa, Rhodesia and Malawi. Portugal herself has plans to settle one million white immigrants in the area which partly explains the policy of clearing the Frelimo from the Tete area in which the massacre at Wiriyamu is alleged to have taken place. For her part South Africa needs a guaranteed local source of oil against the eventuality of a future blockade. Here the presence of a major oilfield at Cabinda,

Angola, assumes considerable significance. To the extent that South Africa herself is economically dependent on the British connection (see Chapter 3) South Africa's involvement is indirectly, but no less effectively, a British involvement.

The reasons for British support for the present Portuguese régime are clearly almost exclusively strategic ones. While Britain herself runs no military bases in metropolitan Portugal, the United States and France maintain bases in the Azores. A third NATO ally, West Germany, maintains an important base at Beja. The crux of Britain's interest in keeping the 600-year-old Anglo-Portuguese alliance in working order rests heavily on maintaining the trade routes open around the Cape. The British Foreign Secretary's concern with the Soviet naval presence in the Indian Ocean is well known. Equally well known is the substantial support given by China to liberation movements in Southern Africa.

Whether continued support for Portugal by the British Government will safeguard Southern Africa from either Soviet or Chinese penetration may well prove a secondary question to the grim fact that Britain is in the meantime shoring up the white supremacists in Southern Africa, not least through her largely uncritical attitudes to Portugal. When France next pushes forward the candidacy of Portugal in Brussels Britain should demand, as part of the price of membership, the liberalisation and gradual run-down of the Portuguese presence in Southern Africa. Any lesser demand will poison the whole future relationship between Africa and Europe besides betraying the peoples of Portugal and Southern Africa. Meanwhile the strategic issues remain probably deliberately clouded.

Southern Africa and Britain's Strategic Interests

In spite of the British Government's avowed disapproval of apartheid the Royal Navy still carries out joint manoeuvres with the South African navy and shares a naval base with them at Simonstown. The official explanation given for this apparently paradoxical situation is that the Soviet naval presence in the Indian Ocean constitutes a threat to British and African interests. Whatever its primary purpose it is also true that the British naval presence on South African soil is a form of military guarantee to the present régime in Pretoria (possibly also to those in Luanda and Lourenco Marques) and a minimal safeguard for British financial interests in the Republic. The question is what is the nature of Britain's strategic interest in Southern Africa?

Importance of Indian Ocean

Unlike the Atlantic and Pacific Oceans, and even the Mediterranean, the Indian Ocean has not always been a high priority military area. Two recent developments, one military and the other geological, have changed all that. First, the capacity of nuclear submarines to operate anywhere in the world. Secondly, the world scarcity of various raw materials. In the countries surrounding the Indian Ocean at least 20 out of the 40 raw materials designated as strategically indispensable are to be found. Among the major natural resources of the region are oil, copper, manganese, asbestos, cotton, sugar and jute. By far the most important resource is oil, mostly from Saudi Arabia, Iran and Kuwait.

Not only does the area provide 30 per cent of the world's current supply of petroleum, but possibly more important, it contains 70 per cent of the world's known reserves. Among the major oil-consuming countries Japan is by far the most dependent (90 per cent) on supplies from the Gulf. But Western Europe as a whole is not far behind with Italy (84 per cent), Britain (66 per cent), West Germany (62 per cent) and France (50 per cent). The United States is, relatively speaking, the least dependent of the Western industrial nations with only 8 per cent from Saudi Arabia. At the moment 70 per cent of this oil flows overland by pipeline to the Mediterranean but everyone now knows that this is an extremely vulnerable means of supply in both political and military terms. Moreover, it has been calculated that the Soviet Union's major oilfield at Baku will have run dry by 1980, which could greatly complicate matters.

Meanwhile, since the closure of the Suez Canal in 1967, vast supertankers of 200,000 tons plus have been ploughing their way round the Cape, an essential lifeline of Western Europe's industrial economy. Since the Suez Canal drew 80 per cent of its revenue from tankers, rarely over 70,000 tons, if the Canal were reopened it would almost certainly need to be drastically enlarged to become a commercial waterway once more. But, like the overland pipelines, the Canal would always remain highly vulnerable in time of war.

Around 98 per cent of Australia's trade with Britain is transported via the Cape, while most of the U.K.–New Zealand trade travels via Panama. One scarcely escape the conclusion that the Cape route is not only strategically very important to most of Western Europe but that it is a trade route that has come to stay. This is even more true since the advent of supertankers and containerisation, with its spectacular increase in the average tonnage of commercial ships which can only use the major Canals when in ballast.

The Soviet Challenge

Ever since Peter the Great conceived the dream of controlling the seas stretching in an arc from the Baltic to the Pacific, Russia has dreamed of patrolling the Indian Ocean. Yet as recently as 1964 the Soviet Union proposed that the Indian Ocean be declared a 'neutral zone'. When this was turned down the Soviet Union began to introduce a naval presence of its own to counter those of Britain, France and the United States. But as with all Soviet policy in Asia, the main intention seems to have been to outflank China. The Anglo-American acquisition of the A3 missile (range: 2,500 miles) for their Polaris and Poseidon submarines has placed the Soviet industrial heartlands within nuclear range of both the Arabian Sea and the Bay of Bengal. Not surprisingly the Soviet Union has steadily increased not only its naval presence but also its merchant marine (operating as an auxiliary arm of its navy) in the Indian Ocean. Today Soviet naval strength is probably greater than that of any other single nation but certainly considerably less than the combined U.S., British and French naval forces. Moreover, in spite of her access to naval facilities on Socotra Island, Aden and Mogadishu (giving her control of the north-western exit to the Indian Ocean) and the right to use the Indian submarine base at Visakhapatnam, the Soviet navy has no permanent base any nearer to the Indian Ocean than Vladivostok! The dispute in which Indonesia and Malaysia ranged themselves against Japan and the Soviet Union over who should control the Straights of Malacca, virtually the eastern exit to the Indian Ocean, only emphasises that the Soviet naval forces are far from dominating the Ocean.

The question remains, is the Soviet Union likely, under any foreseeable circumstances, to attack British commercial shipping in the Indian Ocean? The possibility is extremely remote for at least one very good reason. Namely, the Soviet Union's increasing dependence on foreign trade and the size of her own merchant marine would invite immediate retaliation. Since the Western powers control the Baltic exits, the Dardanelles, Gibraltar and the Tsushima Strait (the only navigable exit from Vladivostok) the Soviet Union seems very unlikely to embark on such a course. The real threat, if threat it is, is Soviet influence in the Third World which arguably can be extended by a discreet, semi-permant naval presence.

If the Soviet Union has gained the greater influence in India, especially since the Indo-Pakistan war over Bangladesh, and in continental southern Asia generally, it is the Chinese, with their non-Caucasian origins, who have gained the firmer foothold in East and Southern Africa, notably in Tanzania and Zambia. The Russians of course remain a powerful influence in both Egypt and Somalia. Yet the available evidence suggests that Soviet activity is almost solely aimed at containing China in Asia and minimising its rivals' influence in Africa. At the moment both China and the Soviet Union enjoy the advantage in both Asia and Africa of being 'anti-colonialist' powers. The reverse side of the coin is also true. Thus as long as Britain and France are seen to support the European dominated governments of Southern Africa they will be regarded as neo-colonialists. Can anything constructive be done to alter Britain's role as the indispenable economic, defence and diplomatic bulwark of the status quo in South Africa?

One of the few possibilities would be for Britain to disassociate herself from the South African military nexus by ceasing to use Simonstown. An alternative way in which to police the Cape would be to expand the facilities at Port Louis, Mauritius, where Britain has a defence agreement up for renewal. As Mauritius has a massive unemployment problem, is almost totally dependent on sugar exports and is well disposed toward Britain there are added reasons for regarding the island as a potential 'mini-Malta' in the Indian Ocean. Since the French are being asked to evacuate their bases on neighbouring Malagasy the expansion of Port Louis could even become a joint Anglo—French undertaking. Together with the U.S. base at Diego Garcia it could be a sufficient toehold to allay fears of a Soviet threat to Europe's trade routes. The gains to me made from openly, if only partially, disengaging from South Africa would be incalculable.

Finally, the discovery of extensive North Sea oilfields may ultimately reduce Britain's dependence on Middle East oil, but it does not remove Britain's and indeed Western Europe's need of other strategic raw materials. In the short term Britain's economic links with Iran are likely to be strengthened.

Postscript: From Affluence to Austerity, 1973

The events which took place throughout the world as an outcome of the 1973 Middle East war telescoped graphically many of the trends which this book has attempted to describe and analyse. Among the issues which these events highlighted is the fragility of the western economic system and the limits to growth built on current sources of energy. The war also illustrated how a single major event can influence each of the world's superblocs, and through them every country on earth, even when the immediate threat of an enlarged war was doused by an early accommodation between the two superpowers. The events of the second half of 1973 almost certainly mark the end of an era of worldwide industrial growth which began around 1950. Among the most fundamental assumptions of this era was that most resources, if not unlimited, would be readily substituted. The 'discovery' that the single most important current source of energy, oil, could become a highly expensive commodity overnight because of its scarcity and the absence of immediate alternatives has made many of the warnings of the environmental lobby come to pass much sooner than expected. The seriousness of this against the background situation described in this book is twofold: first, by causing a series of recessions in the industrialised countries it could feed the protectionist trends which have been gathering momentum for some time; second, by vastly increasing transport costs and favouring local and sometimes inefficient producers, the increase in oil prices will have a worldwide inflationary effect, directly and indirectly.

To foresee the prospect of a world recession accompanied by the twin evils of mass unemployment and acute inflation is in the present climate of events not to be alarmist but merely realistic. Yet the very enormity of the dangers which face the world economic system holds out the challenge of a drastically reformed economic pattern where the nature of growth can be much more widely and severely questioned than hitherto. The issues of environmental economics and of intermediate technology for instance are likely to be translated from the margins of economic concern to a central place in economic policy making, in the medium if not the short term.

From the events flowing from the 1973 Middle East war around five general conclusions can be usefully drawn, broadly corroborated by the evidence surveyed in the main part of the book.

The first is that the energy crisis, by its effect on the industrialised and non-industrialised worlds' pattern of consumption, the rate of inflation and balance of power between the oil producing and oil consuming countries, only underlines a continuing theme of this book — namely the interdependence of the world economic system. It also reveals the general outlines of the superbloc, as sketched in Chapter 3 for instance, with the EEC standing aside from the initial U.S.—Soviet confrontation and seeking preferential treatment from the Arab oil states, i.e. preserving the Eurafrican superbloc alliance. Subsequently, Britain, following in France's footsteps, has sought to negotiate barter deals with the Arab oil states by providing military equipment in return for guaranteed quantities of oil, a characteristic agreement between components of superblocs (witness the many similiar arrangements between the Soviet Union and her East European satellites). A further aspect arising from the energy crisis upon which the superbloc system impinges is that any attempt to create a World Energy Authority would have to embrace nuclear energy, a defence question. Very few of the superblocs, if any, and least of all Japan, look likely to surrender much ground on this most substantive of issues. Meanwhile the need for an energy action committee representing the major western industrial powers acting in concert with the oil producing Arab states together with Iran, Venezuela and Canada to step into the breach must be a high priority.

A second general conclusion would be the accentuated need for a stabilisation of world commodity prices. The extent to which high prices for primary commodities tend to suffer a severe slump following a period of high prices is historically well substantiated. The need for both producer and consumer nations is for stability under a mutually agreed price framework. The present rise in oil prices may conceivably help the Third World's combined bargaining power in the GATT negotiations but it should not be seen to benefit directly more than a very few developing countries. Moreover, its effects have already been severe on most poor countries and can only temporarily be alleviated by aid programmes from the oil states. As a result of the energy shortage the objective of guarantees for the Third World primary exports, and possibly agriculture generally, appears a much more feasible objective in the GATT talks. Should the Third World's worsening plight be ignored then the Malthusian nightmare of population outstripping food production could be savagely fulfilled, particularly if poor harvests coincided in the Soviet Union, China and North America.

A third conclusion is the potential shift in the balance of power between the Soviet and Chinese superblocs and the three western superblocs — the United States, the EEC and Japan. Before the Yom Kippur war the three western superblocs undoubtedly faced a general trade recession in 1974 with ominous signs that (unless arrested by a spectacular measure of agreement in the GATT negotiations) it would grow progressively worse as protectionist policies were increasingly adopted. The war and its aftermath have practically guaranteed a world slump. This will harm Japan, the EEC and the United States severely but the Soviet Union and China hardly at all. Such a slump likely to affect western morale as well as living standards, could give the Soviet Union in particular the kind of advantage in Europe for instance which could call forth a much more hawkish attitute toward the West. The Soviet Union, already the pre-eminent conventional military power in Europe and arguably with a nuclear edge over the United States, could readily become the strongest power economically. From such a position it would be only a short step before the Soviet

Union supplanted the United States as Europe's military as well as economic guarantor without so much as moving a single division or firing a shot. In the Far East, China's remarkable degree of self-sufficiency described earlier, will have greatly strengthened her position relative to that of Japan as a result of the energy crisis.

A fourth conclusion is that as the economic links between the components of the superbloc multiply (e.g. between the Arab states and the EEC) so will the political involvement inevitably expand. If the régime of a particular member of the superbloc is generally repressive then the internal security of its 'partners' in the superbloc becomes at risk. Hence attempts by Moroccan terrorists to apply pressure against their government have been conducted in France and more recently in Britain. In a somewhat different variation of the same theme the assassination of Admiral Carrero Blanco, General Franco's nominated Prime Minister and heir apparent, by Basque nationalists, led to moves against Basque nationalists in south western France. With the French Government anxious to bring Spain into the Community as soon as possible and three quarters of the EEC's largest multinational companies maintaining Spanish subsidiaries or affiliates the destiny of the two countries is closely linked. It is also worth noting that in the case of an as yet evolving superbloc such as Eurafrica the effective capital may not be the nominal one. Thus while Brussels may be the capital of the EEC itself it is Paris that is the capital of Eurafrica, as President Pompidou's calling of the Europe—Arab and Europe—African conference in Salzburg and Dakar respectively forcefully underlines.

In times which promise to be as cataclysmic as any since 1939 or 1929, and as seminal as 1914, one may perhaps be excused for concluding on an entirely personal note. The political and economic forces which I have attempted to describe create a situation of fluidity in world affairs almost without parallel in history. For myself I cannot escape an awareness of what I can only call an 'air of judgement' hanging over European civilisation. Whether one see this as marking the end of an era of profligacy by our bloated western industrial society, when our neglect of the burgeoning undernourished millions of the Third World will be brought to account or whether one sees events, particularly in the Middle East, as taking on an eschatalogical aspect, we cannot escape into the comfort of some unaffected sanctuary. Infatuated by the seemingly unalloyed benefits of economic growth, western industrial society has long since discarded those spiritual, largely Judaeo—Christian, tenets to which in the past our civilisation has turned in periods of crisis. The postwar attempt to recreate Europe as a world power may represent the last unconscious attempt — the First and Second World Wars were the two previous conscious attempts this century — to reassert European power to match its former and still current cultural influence. Such an effort, defying the tides of history in the form of the colossal growth of populations outside Europe and their growing capacity to exploit their natural resources, has also lacked the spiritual conviction which every civilisation needs to galvanise its members. The question which remains to be answered is can western society evolve a socio-economic pattern which will take account of both the world's enormous population growth and its limited resources? The answer to that question lies in my view as much in the rediscovery of the spiritual dimension in man, revolutionising our basic attitudes toward the consumption and sharing of resources, as in the precise modes of husbanding our human as well as our natural resources with which political economy has perforce to confine itself.

Index